In the Umrah
The journey to Madinah Munawwarah

في مَدِينَةِ رَسُولِ اللهِ صَلَّى اللهُ عَلَيْهِ وَسَلَّمْ

In the City of Rasulullah صَلَّى اللهُ عَلَيْهِ وَسَلَّمَ

Published By: Islamic Book Store

فِيْ مَدِيْنَةِ رَسُوْلِ اللَّهِ صَلَّى اللَّهُ عَلَيْهِ وَسَلَّمَ

In the City of Rasulullah ﷺ

فِيْ مَدِيْنَةِ رَسُوْلِ اللَّهِ صَلَّى اللَّهُ عَلَيْهِ وَسَلَّمَ

In the City of Rasulullah ﷺ

Title: In the City of Rasulullah ﷺ

Compiled by:
Jamiatul Ulama (KZN)
Ta'limi Board
4 Third Avenue
P.O.Box 26024
Isipingo Beach
4115
South Africa
Tel: (+27) 31 912 2172
Fax: (+27) 31 902 9268
E-mail: info@talimiboardkzn.org
Website: www.talimiboardkzn.org

Published:
Islamic Book Store
302 Saad Residancy
Sahin Park M G Road
Bardoli Surat Gujarat
India 394601
UDYAM REGISTRATION NUMBER :
UDYAM-GJ-22-0457400

Contents

Introduction i

CHAPTER ONE
Preparation for the blessed Journey 1

CHAPTER TWO
The journey to Madinah Munawwarah 8

CHAPTER THREE
At the Raudha Mubaarak of Rasulullah ﷺ 21

CHAPTER FOUR
Masjidun Nabawi 45

CHAPTER FIVE
Virtues of Madinah Munawwarah 58

CHAPTER SIX
Virtues of Durood & Salaam 75

CHAPTER SEVEN
Jannatul Baqee (The Graveyard of Madinah) 89

CHAPTER EIGHT
Masjidul Quba 108

CHAPTER NINE
Mount Uhud 116

CHAPTER TEN
The Battle of Khandaq (Trench) 158

CHAPTER ELEVEN
Leaving Madinah Munawwarah................................. 176

CHAPTER TWELVE
Poems in praise of our beloved Nabi ﷺ 183

Introduction

All praise is for Allah Ta'ala, our Rabb, our Creator, our Nourisher and our Cherisher. May the special peace and mercy of Allah Ta'ala rain upon our beloved Nabi, Sayyiduna wa Maulana Muhammadur Rasulullah ﷺ.

The best city on the face of the earth is the city of **Madinah Munawwarah**. This is the city of none other than the leader of mankind, the chosen messenger, the beloved of Allah Ta'ala, Ahmad-e-Mujtaba Muhammad-e-Mustafa ﷺ. Allah Ta'ala chose this city to be the special place of residence for His Nabi ﷺ as well as his resting place till the Day of Qiyaamah.

Every Muslim has a deep sense of love and attachment for Madinah Munawwarah and every person desires to visit this mubaarak city over and over again in his short life. He also yearns from the bottom of his heart for death in this noble land, to be buried in the graveyard of Madinah Shareef amongst the 10 000 Sahaabah *(radiyallahu anhum)* who lay buried there. Muslims all over the world spend thousands of dollars just to spend a few days in this blessed city.

Unfortunately, many a time, due to our ignorance, we do not know the significance and virtues of this mubaarak place and come with the wrong mindset and thus do not appreciate our time there. Much of our valuable time is spent in shopping and visiting the malls thus making Madinah Munawwarah into just another holiday destination. (May Allah Ta'ala forgive us for this).

Hadhrat Moulana Maseehullah Khan Saahib *(rahmatullahi alayh)* used to say;

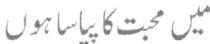

I am thirsty for love

Showing the Ummah that our weakness today is our deficiency in love. Love for who? Love for Allah Ta'ala, love for Nabi Muhammad ﷺ, love for Islam, love for the Sunnah, love for the Sahaabah *(radhiyallahu anhum)*, love for the Ambiyaa *(alayhimus salaam)*, love for the Imaams of Fiqh and Hadith and love for the Muslims in general.

In the past when people visited Madinah Munawwarah, they felt as if a new life was kindled within them. The incidents of Seerat, which they studied in their formative maktab years as little children, suddenly became alive before their eyes. The love for Madinah Munawwarah was strongly embedded in their hearts to this extent that they were prepared to sacrifice everything they had for the beloved city.

The visitor to Madinah felt the great honour of walking on the same ground that his beloved Nabi ﷺ walked on, to breathe in the same air that he breathed and to drink the same water he drank. When one stood infront of the Raudha Mubaarak, his beard would get drenched with his tears. He would be unable to contain himself as he stood there reciting salaat and salaam upon Rasulullah ﷺ. He would feel as if his heart would explode due to his excessive love for Rasulullah ﷺ.

Introduction

What has happened to us now? How is it that we do not have the same yearning anymore? Why do we not experience the same joy which they experienced? What has happened to out hearts? How is it that when the poems of our Akaabir (elders) in praise of Rasulullah ﷺ are read before us, our hearts are not shaken in the least? Is it because our hearts have become heedless of the remembrance of Allah Ta'ala? Is it because of our sins and our arrogance? Is it because we have left the lifestyle of Rasulullah ﷺ and adopted the way of life of his enemies? Is it because we are coming so often that we lost the respect of this sanctified place? May Allah forgive us for our disrespect to this beautiful city and help us fill our hearts with the love of our beloved Nabi ﷺ.

It is with the intention of once again rekindling the spirit of love during our visit to Madinah Shareef that this humble book was compiled. Our beloved and respected ustaaz and shaikh, Hadhrat Mufti Ebraheem Salejee Saahib *(daamat barakaatuhu)*, suggested that a book be prepared which will educate the visitor to the beloved city of the *aadaab* (etiquettes), the virtues and the history of the different sites of Madinah Munawwarah.

He suggested that the book "Wafaaul Wafa" written by Allamah Samhoodi *(rahmatullahi alayh)* be researched for this purpose. The book "Kaarawaan-e-Madeenah" written by Hadhrat Moulana Abul Hasan Ali Nadwi *(rahmatullahi alayh)* was also researched and some aspects from this book were also included. Majority of the content matter has been taken from Fazaail-e-Haj written by Shaikhul Hadith, Hadhrat Moulana Muhammad Zakariyya Kandhlawi *(rahmatullahi alayh)*.

The historical facts have been recorded verbatim from Seeratul Mustafa ﷺ written by Hadhrat Moulana Idrees Kandhlawi *(rahmatullahi alayh)*. Some advices of Hadhrat Mufti Ebraheem Salejee

Saahib *(daamat barakaatuhu)* which were given to his students on his visits to Madinah Munawwarah have also been included.

By the grace of Allah Ta'ala, the commencement of this book took place at the Raudha Mubaarak of Rasulullah ﷺ on the 10th Jumaadus Saani 1438 with the hope that it will gain the special blessings of Rasulullah ﷺ.

The book has been written in the style of a *safar nama*[1]. The book is divided into 12 chapters which are as follows:

1. Preparation for the journey
2. The journey to Madinah Munawwarah
3. The virtues of Madinah Munawwarah
4. The virtues of Masjidun Nabawi
5. The Raudha Mubaarak
6. Virtues of Durood and Salaam
7. Jannatul Baqee (The graveyard of Madinah Shareef)
8. Virtues of Masjid-e-Quba
9. Mount Uhud
10. Sab'ah Masaajid (The place where the Battle of Khandaq was fought)
11. Leaving Madinah Munawwarah
12. Some Arabic and Urdu poems in praise of Rasulullah ﷺ and Madinah Munawwarah

May Allah Ta'ala make this book a means of attaining His special pleasure, His proximity as well as the proximity and pleasure of our

---

[1] Report of a journey undertaken

Introduction

beloved Nabi, Muhammad ﷺ. This, in actual fact, is the ultimate goal of every believer.

Nothing can be achieved without the Grace and Mercy of Allah Ta'ala and for this we seek the help of Allah Ta'ala in all our affairs.

وَالصَّلَاةُ وَالسَّلَامُ عَلٰی اَشْرَفِ الْاَنْبِيَاءِ وَالْمُرْسَلِيْنَ وَعَلٰی اٰلِهِ وَاَصْحَابِهٖ وَ اَتْبَاعِهٖ اَجْمَعِيْنَ

Ta'limi Board (KZN)
Muharram 1440

CHAPTER One

Preparation for the blessed Journey

Visiting the beautiful city of Madinah Munawwarah is indeed a great bounty of Allah Ta'ala upon any ummati. This journey is unlike any other mundane journey that a person undertakes to other destinations of the world. This is a journey to visit the leader of mankind, the beloved of Allah Ta'ala, the master of both the worlds, Hadhrat Nabi Muhammad ﷺ.

Before presenting ourselves in the court of Rasulullah ﷺ in the beautiful city of Madinah Munawwarah, it is extremely necessary for us to first prepare our minds and hearts. The visitor to Madinah Munawwarah should appreciate this great bounty of Allah Ta'ala upon him as an avalanche of sawaab and reward is coming his way.

Many of us, due to the lack of knowledge and preparation, end up ruining our visit to this sacred place and lose all our opportunities to earn millions of rewards.

In the City of Rasulullah ﷺ

Hadhrat Anas رضى الله عنه says that Rasulullah ﷺ left Makkah Mukarramah in such a manner that everything in Makkah became covered in darkness and when he entered Madinah Munawwarah everything became bright and lit up. Nabi ﷺ said:

"My home shall be in Madinah and therein shall be my grave. It is a duty upon every Muslim to visit Madinah."

Thus it is a duty on every Muslim to visit this blessed city. How fortunate indeed is that person who has the great honour to visit Madinah Munawwarah and the Raudha Mubaarak (grave) of Rasulullah ﷺ. Visiting the Raudha Mubaarak (the grave of Rasulullah ﷺ) is the highest of all mustahab actions. The opportunity of presenting oneself in the noble court of our beloved Nabi ﷺ, standing right in front of his grave and reciting durood upon him, is indeed a golden opportunity for us. It is therefore incumbent to first prepare our minds and hearts before reaching Madinah Munawwarah.

Well before leaving for Madinah Shareef, engage in the following;

1. Abundant taubah and istighfaar. Every night before sleeping perform two rakaats Salaatut Taubah and beg Allah Ta'ala to forgive our sins.
2. Make a habit of reciting abundant durood shareef at least a 1000 times every day. This will also increase our yearning and love for Madinah Munawwarah.
3. Plan ourselves properly as to how we will spend our time in this mubaarak city.
4. It is extremely beneficial to listen to the lectures of Hadhrat Moulana Yunus Patel Saahib *(rahmatullahi alayh)* especially the advices he gives to the person going to Madinah Shareef.

Listening to these lectures[1] will *Insha Allah* boost one's spirit and create a deep yearning for visiting the noble city.

5. It is also extremely important for us to read the book, "Fazaail-e-Haj" written by Hadhrat Shaikh Zakariyya (*rahmatullahi alayh*). There are many pertinent advices in this book as well as inspiring incidents that will motivate us to spend our time correctly in Madinah Shareef.

Niyyah (intention) before departure

The intention of the visitor to Madinah Shareef is extremely important. The intention must be specifically visiting the grave of Rasulullah ﷺ to attain the pleasure of Allah Ta'ala. In doing so, one is able to practice on the Hadith wherein Rasulullah ﷺ has said:

"Whoever comes as a visitor to me with no other intention except to visit me, for him shall I surely be an intercessor."

Let this journey be only for Allah's pleasure. There should neither be any *riyaa* (show), or pride, nor should there be any intention of travelling for the sake of touring or sightseeing, and nor should there be any worldly intention (like business, shopping, etc.). If we have other worldly intentions, our sawaab (reward) will be decreased or lost.

Hadhrat Mufti Ebrahim Salehjee Saahib (*daamat barakaatuhu*) always advises those going to the mubaarak lands to make intention for *islaah* (reformation) and *muhabbat* (love). We must make *niyyat* (intention) to change our lives and return as better Muslims, practicing on the Sunnah of Rasulullah ﷺ in everything we do or say.

---

[1] *These lectures can be downloaded from the website www.yunuspatel.co.za*

Valuable advices for the visitor to Madinah Munawwarah

1. Carry along with you a few suitcases of Sabar (patience).
2. Leave behind (i.e. at home) three things:
    a. Anger.
    b. Expectations & comfort.
    c. Anxiety and panic.
3. Always maintain a smiling face.
4. Restrain your anger. Do not quarrel or fight with anyone, though it may be their fault.
5. Do not engage in *gheebah* (back-biting) at all. This will nullify the reward of all your efforts.
6. As far as possible, avoid the company of people you know without hurting their feelings. Much time is wasted in this way.
7. Remain in the state of wudhu at all times.
8. Give sadaqah daily even if it is one riyaal.
9. Try your best not to miss any salaah with jamaat and takbeer-e-Ula in Masjidun Nabawi. Plan your trip such that you will be able to performe at least 40 Salaahs in Masjidun Nabawi.
10. Ensure that you perform all your Nafal and Sunnah Salaah in these blessed lands. Be regular with Chaast, Ishraaq, Awwaabeen and also the Sunnats and Nafal Salaah before and after the Faraaidh.
11. Do not take any pictures of the Green Dome or the masjid on your cell phone. It may amount to disrespect. Many people take pictures of themselves (selfies) in the Haram Shareef. This is totally impermissible.
12. Speak with respect to the police and officials.
13. Do not speak anything against the people of Madinah.

14. Wish well for everyone and have a good opinion about all Muslims in general.
15. Don't make a point of looking out for the wrongs of people. If you come across anyone doing a wrong, make dua for your and their forgiveness.
16. At all times try and make this dua in your heart, "O Allah! Protect me, correct me and guide me".
17. Drink as much Zam Zam as possible.
18. Do not waste your valuable time in shopping. Remember the worst of places is the bazaar.
19. Remember to guard the two T's. Your Tongue and your Time.
20. Draw up a daily programme for yourself i.e. how many paras tilaawat, zikr, Hizbul A'zam, nafal salaah, dua, etc. you will be reciting daily. Thereafter follow the program diligently.
21. On the flight, engage in zikr, tilaawat, or reading of some authentic Islamic book. Do not read the "In flight magazine."
22. Prepare a list of duas as well as a list of people for whom you will make dua for in the Haram Shareef and other sanctified places.
23. The greatest ibaadat is *adab* (respect) and *muhabbat* (love). Respect for Allah Ta'ala, His Nabi ﷺ, the mubaarak city, respect for the inhabitants of the city, respect for the masjid, respect for the Qur-aan Shareef, respect for old and weak people, respect for all Muslims in general.

Travel Tips

1. Travel as light as possible.
2. Have a shawl with you at all times. (can be used for salaah, blanket, dastarkhan, etc.)
3. Carry one set of clothing in your hand luggage. It will come in handy in the event of luggage getting lost.
4. Check if the toilet and bed in your hotel room is facing the Qiblah or not. Many a times the toilets and beds do face the Qiblah. Be careful in this regard. If the toilet is facing the Qiblah, sit on the seat in such a way that you are not facing the Qiblah
5. Carry a shoe bag to the Haram Shareef.
6. Take sufficient amount of padkos (food for the journey). Do not take extra, because it gets wasted.
7. Carry a pocket size Hizbul A'zam / Munajaat Maqbul and 40 durood and salaam to recite daily.

List of things to take along

1. Travel documents (passports, tickets, injection cards, currency). Double and triple check before leaving
2. Keep copies of passports and visas with you as well as a copy of these documents at home
3. Clothes (5 sets is sufficient)
4. Towels
5. Shoe bag for haram
6. Itr (apply especially when going to the Raudha Mubaarak)
7. Tawaaf tasbeeh
8. Ihraam
9. Ihraam sandal
10. Ihram belt

11. Vest with pockets for money
12. Cosmetic bag with nail clipper, soap, toothbrush, tooth paste etc. (Not to take in hand luggage)
13. Non-perishable foods. Dry snacks like chips, biscuits, rusks, etc.
14. Pen, diary, pocket notebook
15. Miswaak
16. Wrist watch
17. Basic medication – Panado, etc.
18. Mozas
19. Small pocket / utility knife (not in hand luggage)
20. Dastarkhan, paper plates and cups
21. Food (Not too much)

CHAPTER Two

The journey to Madinah Munawwarah

At the airport

In this day and age, we use the facilties at the airports and in the planes when travelling for Umrah and Haj. At the same time we know very well that these are places of immense fitnah and evil. Sin and wrong invites a person from all directions. Music, women, adverts, bill boards are glaring into the faces of the travellers, diverting their attention from Allah Ta'ala and His beloved Nabi ﷺ. One has to exercise great caution in these places.

Hadhrat Mufti Ebrahim Salehjee Saahib *(daamat barakaatuhu)* would strongly discourage fellow travellers from walking around freely and spending their time shopping and loitering at the airports. He would say that this will distract our minds from the purpose for which one is undertaking the journey. He himself would sit in a corner and remain engaged in the tilaawat of the Qur-aan-e-Kareem or the recitation of Durood Shareef.

At the time of salaah, he would ask one of the saathies (companions) to call out the azaan loudly irrespective of which airport it was and would instruct us to perform salaah in the open saying that calling out the azaan and performing salaah in the open is a strong da'wat for the non-Muslims and also a reminder for the Muslims.

We also noticed Hadhrat Mufti Saahib *(daamat barakaatuhu)* adopting calmness in the airports. He never hurried or rushed to go through the procedures. His eyes would always be focused on his companions, checking that everything and everyone was okay whilst his tongue would be constantly engaged in the tilaawat of the Quraan-e-Majeed.

In the aircraft

In the aircraft also, one has to be very careful. Fitnahs abound from all sides. Scantily dressed women present themselves to you and one has to be extremely careful of one's eyes, ears and heart. The TV screen in front of you is extremely tempting. Latest videos and movies are available at the press of a button. Music blares loudly leaving a person with no choice but to block his ears with his fingers. The visitor to Madinah Munawwarah has to be extra cautious whilst travelling, making sure that his heart is not tainted with any evil before presenting himself in the court of Rasulullah ﷺ.

We noticed that Hadhrat Mufti Saahib *(daamat barakaatuhu)* would be very cautious when entering the plane ensuring that he does not come into contact with any females especially the hostess standing at the entrances. He would keep his gaze lowered and would keep his tongue busy with the tilaawat of the Qur-aan Shareef. When sitting, he would prefer not to sit on an aisle seat so as to have the least amount of contact with the hostesses moving up and down the aisle. Most of the time he would sit with his gaze lowered and would not even lift up his head to see what's happening inside the aircraft. The moment he sat down, he took a blanket and covered the television screen in front of him so as not to even look at it by mistake. At night, he would spend much of his time performing Tahajjud Salaah on his seat.

At the time of salaah, Hadhrat would quickly stand up and perform his salaah in a corner of the plane. He would advise us not to cause any inconvenience to fellow passengers when performing salaah and when making wudhu. He would say that when it is a public facility we should be considerate to others and make wudhu as quickly as possible. On one occasion he advised us that the tasbeehaat and duas read in salaah should be shortened in the plane. Hadhrat Mufti Saahib *(daamat barakaatuhu)* was also very particular about performing salaah with jamaat in the plane. He advised us to pair ourselves and perform all our salaah with jamaat so as to gain maximum reward.

Approaching Madinah Munawwarah

دل تڑپتا ہے میرا سینے میں ہائے پہنچوں گا کب مدینے میں

My heart is restless, when will I reach Madinah?

It took some time at the airport to complete the immigration. Some of us began getting edgy and frustrated due to the long lines and the time it was taking to get through. Hadhrat Mufti Saahib *(daamat barakaatuhu)* advised us to be tolerant and to have patience. He explained that our presence in the airport of Madinah Shareef was indeed a great bounty of

Allah Ta'ala for which we were undeserving. He advised us to be grateful and ponder over the fact that we were not worthy of being even in the airport of such a noble city.

After stamping our passports, we left the airport and boarded a small bus that took us to our hotel. On the way, Hadhrat Mufti Saahib *(daamat barakaatuhu)* advised us to focus our minds and busy ourselves in the recitation of Durood Shareef.

Hadhrat Shaikhul Hadeeth, Moulana Muhammad Zakariyya *(rahmatullahi alayh)* has advised us in his famous book, Fazaail-e-Durood that as we approach Madinah Munawwarah, it is excellent for us to read durood shareef abundantly the moment we see the trees and buildings of Madinah Munawwarah. With fervor and love one should increase his durood, for these are the places where the Qur-aan Shareef was revealed. Hadhrat Jibraeel *(alayhis salaam)* and Hadhrat Mikaaeel *(alayhis salaam)* frequented this place and the blessed soil of Madinah Munawwarah contains the leader of mankind, Nabi Muhammad ﷺ. From here the religion of Islam and the sunnah of Rasulullah ﷺ spread. This is the home of all good and virtue. When you come to Madinah Munawwarah, you should be full of fear and respect, as though you are going to meet Rasulullah ﷺ himself for it is definite that Rasulullah ﷺ will hear your salaams.

How fortunate am I, (my good fortune) that I am making Tawaaf of your house., Am I awake or is this a dream?

Travel with great hope and excitement and increase the yearning within you as Madinah Munawwarah draws closer. In order to increase that excitement, we should read some poems about Rasulullah ﷺ.[1] If a book about Rasulullah ﷺ is available, read it or have it read for others to listen to, so that the life of Rasulullah ﷺ is discussed and all thoughts are about him, so much so that when the day of entering Madinah Munawwarah is near, the longing should be at its peak.

When along the way you pass those places or masaajid about which it is known that Rasulullah ﷺ or his Sahaabah *(radiyallahu anhum)* had rested or performed salaah therein, then stop there to perform nafal salaah or keep busy with the recitation of durood shareef. Similarly when passing any wells, drink the water for the sake of *barakah* (blessings). Find out where these places are and make a point of stopping there. Among these places there is one special place called Muarras, which is near Zhul-Hulaifa just outside Madinah Munawwarah. Here we should definitely stop and perform Salaah. Some Ulama say that it is Sunnatul-Muakkadah, i.e. a very important sunnah[2].

When nearing Madinah Munawwarah, our enthusiasm and excitement should be at its highest. Salawaat (Durood) should be read very often. If you are on the back of a horse or camel, you should try to ride it faster. It is reported that whenever Rasulullah ﷺ returned from a journey and approached Madinah Munawwarah, he rode his camel faster (over the last stretch).

---

[1] *Some poems have been included at the end of this book*
[2] *Hadhrat Imaam Maalik (rahmatullahi alayh) would make sure he stopped here to perform two rakaats salaah.*

Finally we will see the boundaries of Madinah Munawwarah. Then, when we see the trees of Madinah Munawwarah when passing Bi'r Ali, it is best to come out from our vehicles and continue barefoot towards the city with tears flowing from our eyes, and Salawaat (Durood) flowing from our lips. It used to be the habit of the kings and rulers that they would go walking from Zhul-Hulaifa, which is about ten kilometres from Madinah Munawwarah.

NB: This is only for those who are strong and can easily manage. As for weak people like us, there is no problem if we enter Madinah Munawwarah by car.

When you are about to enter Madinah Munawwarah, read Salawaat (Durood) and the following dua:

اَللّٰهُمَّ هٰذَا حَرَمُ نَبِيِّكَ فَاجْعَلْهُ لِيْ وِقَايَةً مِّنَ النَّارِ وَأَمَانًا مِّنَ الْعَذَابِ وَسُوْءِ الْحِسَابِ

O Allah, this is the Haram of Your Nabi ﷺ. Let it be for me a means of safety from the fire of Jahannam, a safety from punishment and a safety from the difficulty of the questioning.

Then make dua for getting the *barakah* (blessings) of the Blessed City, for the strength to respect Madinah Munawwarah, and for help to stay away from all things that are makrooh (disliked).

At all times think of the sanctity of the city of Madinah Munawwarah because this is the place chosen by Allah Ta'ala for His beloved Rasul ﷺ after he migrated from Makkah Mukarramah. This is the place where Rasulullah ﷺ used to walk, where the Qur-aan Shareef was revealed, where the greatest lectures and talks took place and the most valuable advises given.

In the City of Rasulullah ﷺ

When you first see Madinah Munawwarah, think that this is the city which Allah Ta'ala had chosen for His messenger ﷺ. This is the city where Allah Ta'ala revealed to him the fardh (compulsory) duties of a Muslim. He explained the sunnats of His Deen and here is the place from where he had to fight against the enemies. Here is the place where his Deen became victorious and here he made an effort until he passed away. Here he and his two friends are buried. At every step, you will find the spots where his feet once stood. While you are walking, step lightly in a respectful manner thinking that you are now walking on the soil where the feet of Rasulullah ﷺ walked. Try to walk like how he used to walk. Think about the time when the Sahaabah (*radiyallahu anhum*) used to be with Rasulullah ﷺ looking at him, listening to him and learning from him. Feel afraid of your sins and misdeeds. Think about how you will present yourself before Nabi ﷺ. Beg Allah Ta'ala for forgiveness before coming in front of Rasulullah ﷺ. Ask Allah Ta'ala to hide your sins from Nabi ﷺ.

Upon entering Madinah Munawwarah, we should read the correct duas for this occasion and enter with complete humility.[1] The heart should be distressed for not having visited Rasulullah ﷺ before this and we should be full of hope of meeting him in the hereafter while fearing the worst. We should realise that we are about to come to a very great personality. We should remember his high position and his honour and durood should flow from our lips.

---

[1] *The following is the masnoon dua to read when entering any city:*

اَللّٰهُمَّ بَارِكْ لَنَا فِيْهَا اَللّٰهُمَّ ارْزُقْنَا جَنَاهَا وَ حَبِّبْنَا اِلٰى اَهْلِهَا وَ حَبِّبْ صَالِحِيْ اَهْلِهَا اِلَيْنَا

O Allah! Grant us barakat in this place. O Allah! Give us (to eat) of its produce and make us beloved to its people and create the love of its pious people in us.

When we see the Green Dome of the masjid, we should again remember the honoured and esteemed position of Nabi ﷺ. Remember who is buried beneath that Dome. He who is higher than any other human, the king of all Ambiyaa, he who is higher than even the angels. His grave is more honoured than any part of the earth and the ground on which his noble body lies is even more noble than the Ka'bah Shareef itself, even more noble than the throne (arsh), the kursi (chair of Allah Ta'ala), much more noble than any other place in the heaven or the earth.

After entering the city, go straight to the masjid. (When you have women or luggage with you, then the procedure is different). The Ulama have said that we should first visit the masjid. In fact this was the practice of Nabi ﷺ himself that whenever he returned from a journey, he first went to the masjid.

As for women, when they enter Madinah Munawwarah during the day, it is best that they wait till the night before making ziyaarah, because it is necessary for them to observe the laws of purdah at all times.[1]

Entering Madinah Munawwarah

تمنا ہے کہ گلزارِ مدینہ اب وطن ہوتا ۔ وہاں کے گلشنوں میں کوئی اپنا بھی چمن ہوتا

How I wish Madinah was my home, And that I had my own little garden in the gardens of Madinah.

---

[1] Fazaail-e-Haj

The drive from the airport towards Masjidun Nabawi is a journey of great excitement and anxiety. Hadhrat Mufti Saahib *(daamat barakaatuhu)* advised us to remain engaged in the recitation of Durood Shareef as we travelled towards the Haram Shareef.

We reached our hotel and quickly off-loaded our luggage. Hadhrat Mufti Saahib *(daamat barakaatuhu)* advised us to make ghusal and wear our best clothes. Hadhrat Mufti Saahib *(daamat barakaatuhu)* also made ghusal and wore a brand new set of clothing. He then asked for a comb and combed his beard and hair saying, "Dress neatly. We are going to present ourselves in front of Rasulullah ﷺ. The Sahaabah *(radiyallahu anhum)* were also particular about being neat and clean before they would come to meet Nabi ﷺ. Shouldn't we also present ourselves in a clean and neat manner? We should prepare ourselves as we would on the day of Eid." He also mentioned the following incident;

"Once, a group of people from the family of Abdul Qais came to visit Rasulullah ﷺ in Madinah Munawwarah. When they entered Madinah Munawwarah, they saw Rasulullah ﷺ and immediately became very happy and excited. They jumped off their camels and ran to meet him. Their leader, Munzir bin Aa'iz, who was also called the Shaikh of Abdul Qais, did not follow them. Instead he led their camels to the resting-place, gathered all their goods and placed everything under care. Thereafter he bathed himself, put on his new clothes and slowly went to the masjid with dignity and humility. After entering the masjid he first performed two rakaats Tahiyyatul Masjid, lifted his hands in dua to Allah Ta'ala and then came to Nabi ﷺ. Nabi ﷺ was greatly pleased with him and said; 'There are two qualities in you which are most beloved to Allah, tolerance and dignity.'"

Hadhrat Shaikhul Hadith *(rahmatullahi alayh)* writes that at the time of entering Madinah Munawwarah, have hope that just as Allah Ta'ala had brought you from so far right to the door of Rasulullah ﷺ, Allah Ta'ala in His infinite mercy will allow you to also be with Rasulullah ﷺ in the Aakhirah.

May Allah Ta'ala bless us all with the companionship of Rasulullah ﷺ in Jannah. *Aameen.*

اَللّٰهُمَّ اِنِّيْ اَسْاَلُكَ مُرَافَقَةَ نَبِيِّنَا مُحَمَّدٍ صَلَّى اللهُ عَلَيْهِ وَسَلَّمَ فِيْ اَعْلٰى دَرَجَةِ الْجَنَّةِ جَنَّةِ الْخُلْدِ

O Allah, I beg of You to bless me with the company of our beloved Nabi Muhammad ﷺ in the highest stages of the Everlasting Jannah

جمال کو ترے کب پہنچے حسنِ یوسف کا   وہ دلربائے زلیخا تو شاہدِ ستار

Never will the beauty of Yusuf عَلَيْهِ السَّلَام approach your shining countenance, even though Zulaikha had been bewitched thereby

Towards the Haram Shareef

After applying itr, we left the hotel and began walking towards the Haram Shareef. What a beautiful sight it was. The beautiful minarets of Masjidun Nabawi towered over us and the peace and serenity of this beautiful city gripped our hearts. We couldn't believe that we really were there. The excitement increased as we reached closer to the masjid of Rasulullah ﷺ. Hadhrat Mufti Saahib *(daamat barakaatuhu)* turned around and quietly instructed us to give out some sadaqah before entering the masjid.[1] Hence we gave out some sadaqah and then entered the masjid.

نسیم صباح یہ تیری مہربانی   کہاں میں اور کہاں یہ نکہتِ گل

There is no comparison between me and this fragrant rose, O Rabb of the easterly wind, this is only Your favour

As we entered the Haram Shareef, our hearts began pounding with joy. The beauty of the Masjid of Rasulullah ﷺ engulfed our hearts and minds. Every part of this Masjid is filled with beauty and magnificence and why shouldn't it be so when this is the Masjid of none other than the leader of all of mankind Sayyiduna Muhammadur Rasulullah ﷺ. At first it seemed like a dream but when we got closer to the front of the radiant masjid, we realised this was no dream. We really were there and were about to present ourselves in the court of the master of both the worlds, Sayyiduna wa Habibuna wa Shafiuna wa Maulana Muhammadur Rasulullah ﷺ. We entered the Masjid with the right foot reciting the masnoon dua and salawaat upon Rasulullah ﷺ;

اَللّٰهُمَّ افْتَحْ لِيْ اَبْوَابَ رَحْمَتِكَ

O Allah, open for me the doors of Your mercy

بِسْمِ اللهِ وَالصَّلٰوةُ وَالسَّلَامُ عَلٰى رَسُوْلِ اللهِ

---

[1] Haji Ahmad Nakooda Saahib (db) of Madinah Munawwarah advised that the workers outside the Haram Shareef are deserving of our sadaqah.

and made niyyat for nafal I'tikaaf. Our elders have advised that in the Masjid of Rasulullah ﷺ one must always remain humble and full of respect. One should not worry about the decorations of the masjid, the carpets, pillars, lights, etc. One should go respectfully, keeping one's gaze down and being cautious not to do anything disrespectful.

> *How wonderful is this day, will I ever be able to show my appreciation to my Rabb, my soul has become restless in my chest to fly into the midst of the Raudha Mubaarak*

As we drew closer to the front of the masjid, the *khuddaam* (helpers) of the Haram Shareef began dropping the screens that separate the men from the women. The time for Asar was now getting closer and this gave us an ideal opportunity to move quickly towards the front of the masjid. Hadhrat Mufti Saahib *(daamat barakaatuhu)* indicated to us to perform two rakaats of salaah with the intention of Tahiyyatul Masjid as well as the intention of Salaatush Shukar, thanking Allah Ta'ala for bringing us to this noble land despite us not being worthy of being there. We could not contain our excitement. How aptly the poet mentioned;

اگر فردوس بَر رُوۓ زمین است   ہمین است و ہمین است و ہمین است

If Jannah (paradise) had to be on the face of this earth. Then this is Jannah, this is Jannah, this is Jannah

Every spot of earth in this masjid signifies virtue and greatness. How many of the Sahaabah *(radiyallahu anhum)*, how many of the Awliyaa walked on this land, rather every spot here marks the place where Rasulullah ﷺ placed his mubaarak feet.

Hadhrat Imaam Maalik *(rahmatullahi alayh)* had so much of respect for Madinah Shareef that he never walked on the ground of Madinah Munawwarah with shoes out of respect for this blessed earth.

It is with this frame of mind that we should walk on the ground of Madinah Munawwarah and in Masjidun Nabawi, feeling that we are not worthy of walking on this piece of earth, hoping that every step of ours will be accepted by Allah Ta'ala.

CHAPTER Three

At the Raudha Mubaarak of Rasulullah ﷺ

آ گیا سامنے روضہ محترم   جس کی زیارت کو یا رب ترستے تھے ہم

*We have now come in front of the Raudha Mubaarak,
How enthusiastically we were pining to visit this place O my Rabb*

The highlight of a person's visit to Madinah Munawwarah is the opportunity of presenting oneself at the Raudha Mubaarak of Rasulullah ﷺ. This is that place on the face of this earth which is more virtuous than even the Ka'bah Shareef. Here is the mubaarak residence of Rasulullah

ﷺ. Nabi ﷺ is aware of every person who visits him and replies to their salaams.

After performing Salaah and making dua to Allah Ta'ala to accept our presence in the court of Rasulullah ﷺ, we slowly and respectfully stood up and began edging forward towards the Raudha Mubaarak of Rasulullah ﷺ. We could not contain ourselves as we stood in front of the Raudha Mubaarak reciting;

$$\text{اَلصَّلٰوةُ وَالسَّلَامُ عَلَيْكَ يَا رَسُوْلَ اللهِ}$$

$$\text{اَلصَّلٰوةُ وَالسَّلَامُ عَلَيْكَ يَا حَبِيْبَ اللهِ}$$

$$\text{اَلصَّلٰوةُ وَالسَّلَامُ عَلَيْكَ يَا خَيْرَ خَلْقِ اللهِ}$$

> "Assalaatu wassalaamu alayka ya Rasulullah" (peace and salutations be upon you o Rasulullah ﷺ)
> "Assalaatu wassalaamu alayka ya HabeebAllah" (peace and salutations be upon you o the beloved of Allah ﷺ)
> "As Salaatu wassalaamu alayka ya khaira khalqillah" (peace and salutations be upon you o the best of Allah's creation ﷺ)

The thought of being right in front of Rasulullah ﷺ overwhelmed our minds and hearts. The Hadith of Nabi ﷺ answering our salaam was foremost in our minds. It felt as if our hearts may explode with ecstasy. Which of the favours of Allah Ta'ala can we deny? Such weak individuals, with weak Imaan and weak aa'maal standing in front of the greatest of mankind, Allahu Akbar! How fortunate were we? How fortunate indeed!

یا رب تو کریمی و رسول تو کریم، صد شکر کہ ہستیم میان دو کریم

O my Rabh! You are Kareem and Your Rasul ﷺ is also Kareem (benevolent), how fortunate am I, that I am between two Kareems

At that moment the following dua entered our hearts, "O Allah! bless us with this favour of presenting ourselves in the court of your beloved Rasul ﷺ over and over again. O Allah, even though we are not worthy of being here, shower us with Your Kindness and Mercy and allow us to value every moment of ours in this mubaarak city. O Allah, bless us with a deep sense of love for Rasulullah ﷺ and to become punctual on every sunnah of Rasulullah ﷺ."

O visitor of Madinah, you are about to present yourself in the presence of the greatest of mankind, the most beloved creation of Allah Ta'ala, Nabi Muhammad Mustafa ﷺ. As you walk towards the Raudha Mubaarak keep your heart and mind clear of any bad thoughts. Think only about the great position of Rasulullah ﷺ. The Ulama inform us that the heart of a person will not be blessed with the *barakah* (blessings) of this Noble Place, if it is not free from evil thoughts. In fact, the anger of Rasulullah ﷺ may fall on that person and on the day of Qiyaamah, Nabi ﷺ may turn his mubaarak face away from him. May Allah Ta'ala, through His infinite mercy save us.

It is for this reason that the visitor to the grave of Rasulullah ﷺ should keep his mind free of any worldly needs as much as possible whilst at the same time hoping for Allah's perfect grace. Every visitor should turn his attention to Nabi ﷺ who is a 'mercy to all'. Through his *waseelah* (means), beg Allah's mercy and forgiveness.

In the City of Rasulullah

يَا صَاحِبَ الْجَمَالِ وَيَا سَيِّدَ الْبَشَرْ بِوَجْهِكَ الْمُنِيْرِ لَقَدْ نُوِّرَ الْقَمَرْ

لَا يُمْكِنُ الثَّنَاءُ كَمَا كَانَ حَقُّهُ بعد از خدا بزرگ توئی قصه مختصر

O the possessor of beauty! O the leader of mankind! By your illuminated countenance has the moon found its light. It is not possible to praise you according to your right. After Allah Ta'ala, you are the greatest and that's it.

Presenting one's Salaam

اَحْسَنَ مِنْكَ لَمْ تَرَ قَطُّ عَيْنِيْ وَاَجْمَلَ مِنْكَ لَمْ تَلِدِ النِّسَاءُ

خُلِقْتَ مُبَرَّءًا مِنْ كُلِّ عَيْبٍ كَاَنَّكَ قَدْ خُلِقْتَ كَمَا تَشَاءُ

Better than you no eye has ever seen, more beautiful than you no woman has given birth to

You have been created free from any defect, as if you were created like how you desired

When facing the grave, stand with your back towards the Qiblah, a few steps away from the big brass ring that is on the brass gates at the head side, turning slightly to the right so that your face is exactly opposite the blessed countenance of Rasulullah ﷺ.

Out of respect, do not come nearer, look down, do not look around from side to side. Stand still. Remember that now you are standing facing the mubaarak Rasul of Allah ﷺ and that he knows that you are standing there.

Whilst standing there, make salaam to Rasulullah ﷺ.

At the Raudha Mubaarak of Rasulullah

Hadhrat Moulana Muhammad Zakariyya Saahib *(rahmatullahi alayh)* advises that if one understands Arabic, then one may read the lengthy durood and salaam, pondering over the meanings, but if one does not know the translation, it is better not to read the long duroods from a book. It will be better to stand respectfully, reciting salawaat quietly and slowly in the following words:

اَلصَّلٰوةُ وَالسَّلَامُ عَلَيْكَ يَا رَسُوْلَ اللهِ

"Assalaatu wassalaamu alayka ya Rasulallah"
(Salaat and Salaam be upon you O Rasul of Allah)

Be very careful at the time of reciting salaam, do not shout. The voice should neither be too loud nor too soft. Think about what is being read and feel ashamed of your sins as you stand before Rasulullah ﷺ.

اے خدا اِس بندہ را رُسوا مکن   گربدم من سر من پیدا مکن

O Allah! Don't disgrace this servant of yours, even though I am a sinner, don't expose my sins

اگر چہ پُر خطا ہے پر کہاں جائے تیرا بندہ ، تیرے درپر تیرا بندہ بأُمید کرم آیا

Though I am so sinful O Allah, but where else can I go to? Your slave has come to your doorstep with lots of hope

After greeting Nabi ﷺ, make dua to Allah Ta'ala through the name of Rasulullah ﷺ. Beg for the intercession of Rasulullah ﷺ.

In the City of Rasulullah ﷺ

$$\text{هُوَ الْحَبِيْبُ الَّذِيْ تُرْجٰى شَفَاعَتُهُ لِكُلِّ هَوْلٍ مِّنَ الْأَهْوَالِ مُقْتَحِمِ}$$

He ﷺ is the most beloved (of Allah Almighty) whose intercession is hoped for every fear (and distress) that is going to come (on the day of agony and fears).

After completing one's salaam, read the following dua at the grave of Nabi ﷺ:

$$\text{اَللّٰهُمَّ اِنَّكَ قُلْتَ – وَقَوْلُكَ الْحَقُّ – وَلَوْ أَنَّهُمْ اِذْ ظَلَمُوْا أَنْفُسَهُمْ جَاؤُوْكَ فَاسْتَغْفَرُوْا اللهَ وَاسْتَغْفَرَ لَهُمُ الرَّسُوْلُ لَوَجَدُوا اللهَ تَوَّابًا رَّحِيْمًا , وَقَدْ أَتَيْتُكَ مُسْتَغْفِرًا مِّنْ ذُنُوْبِيْ مُسْتَشْفِعًا بِكَ اِلٰى رَبِّيْ , فَأَسْأَلُكَ يَا رَبِّ أَنْ تُوْجِبَ لِيَ الْمَغْفِرَةَ كَمَا أَوْجَبْتَهَا لِمَنْ أَتَاهُ فِيْ حَيَاتِهٖ}$$

"O Allah, Your word is the truth, and You did say: When they who wrong themselves (by doing sins), come to you and ask for Allah's forgiveness, and the Rasul begs forgiveness for them, then surely they will find Allah Most Forgiving, Most Merciful.' And now I have come to you O Rasulullah ﷺ, asking for forgiveness for my sins, begging you to intercede for me in the presence of Allah and I ask You O Allah to forgive me just like how You had forgiven those who came to Rasulullah ﷺ in his lifetime."

It is mentioned regarding Hadhrat Moulana Husain Ahmad Madani (rahmatullahi alayh) that towards the end of his life he made Haj and when standing in front of the Raudha Mubaarak, he spent three hours

At the Raudha Mubaarak of Rasulullah ﷺ

before the Muwaajah-e-Shareefah (the front section) and burst into tears as he stood conveying salaams to our beloved Rasul ﷺ.

جو تو ہی ہم کو نہ پوچھے تو کون پوچھے گا ۔۔۔ بنے گا کون ہمارا ترے سوا غم خوار

If you do not care for us, then who shall? And who besides you, can truly console us all?

يَا خَيْرَ مَنْ دُفِنَتْ بِالْقَاعِ أَعْظُمُهُ ۔۔۔ فَطَابَ مِنْ طِيْبِهِنَّ الْقَاعُ وَالْأَكَمُ

O the best of all those who have been buried in the earth, because of which the land and the hills have been blessed

نَفْسِي الْفِدَاءُ لِقَبْرٍ أَنْتَ سَاكِنُهُ ۔۔۔ فِيْهِ الْعَفَافُ وَ فِيْهِ الْجُوْدُ وَالْكَرَمُ

May my life be sacrificed for that grave! Where you are lying, there-in lies virtue, generosity and goodness

Forgiveness in front of the Raudha Mubaarak

Once, a villager stood in front of the grave of Rasulullah ﷺ saying: "O Allah, here lies Your beloved, I am Your slave and shaytaan is Your enemy. If You forgive me, Your beloved Nabi ﷺ will become happy. Your slave will be successful, and the heart of Your enemy will be disturbed. O Allah, if You do not forgive me, the heart of Your beloved will be sad, your enemy will be overjoyed and Your slave will fail. O Allah, it is a habit among the Arabs that whenever a great king passes away, they used to free slaves besides his grave. O Allah, here

In the City of Rasulullah

rests the greatest of all kings and here I stand. Please free me, O Allah, from the fire of Jahannam." [1]

Use this opportunity of standing at the Raudha Mubaarak to beg Allah Ta'ala for forgiveness.

تو بہترین خلائق، میں بدترین جہاں   تو سرورِ دو جہاں، میں کمینہ خدمتگار

While the best of creation you are, the worst am I, and while master of both worlds you are, the lowest am I

Sayyid Ahmad Rifaa'ee at the Raudha Mubaarak

Hadhrat Sayyid Ahmad Rifaa'ee *(rahimahullah)* is well known as one of the greatest saints and buzrugs of Islam. In the year 555 A.H. he went for Haj. Thereafter he visited Madinah Munawwarah and whilst standing in front of the grave of Rasulullah ﷺ he read the following poem:

فِيْ حَالَةِ الْبُعْدِ رُوْحِيْ كُنْتُ اُرْسِلُهَا   تُقَبِّلُ الْأَرْضَ عَنِّيْ وَهْيَ نَائِبَتِيْ

وَهٰذِهِ دَوْلَةُ الْأَشْبَاهِ قَدْ حَضَرَتْ   فَامْدُدْ يَمِيْنَكَ كَيْ تَحْظٰى بِهَا شَفَتِيْ

"Before, I used to send my salaams to you O Rasulullah ﷺ from far away, but now I have come myself to greet you. Give me your hand so that my lips may kiss it."

---

[1] *Fazaail-e-Haj*

At the Raudha Mubaarak of Rasulullah

Behold, the hand of Rasulullah ﷺ stretched from the grave and in the presence of an estimated 90 000 visitors did Sayyid Ahmad Rifaa'ee *(rahimahullah)* kiss it.[1]

General advice for those visiting the Raudha Mubaarak

In Fazaail-e-Haj the following advices have been given to the one visiting the Raudha Mubaarak;

Dua

The visitor to the grave of Rasulullah ﷺ should make lots of dua to Allah Ta'ala using the *waseelah* of Rasulullah ﷺ and should beg his intercession because Rasulullah ﷺ is so beloved to Allah Ta'ala that when he intercedes on behalf of anyone, Allah Ta'ala accepts his intercession. You can also make the following dua:

يَا رَسُوْلَ اللهِ أَسْأَلُكَ الشَّفَاعَةَ وَأَتَوَسَّلُ بِكَ اِلَى اللهِ فِيْ أَنْ أَمُوْتَ مُسْلِمًا عَلٰى مِلَّتِكَ وَسُنَّتِكَ

"O Rasulullah ﷺ, I beg your intercession and through you I beg of Allah to let me die as a Muslim on the religion brought by you and in the way taught by you."

While making dua over here, the face should be turned towards Rasulullah ﷺ. If over here we will face the Qiblah whilst making

---

[1] Ibid

dua, then our backs will be towards Rasulullah ﷺ which will be very disrespectful. Therefore dua should be made facing him.

Once, Khalifah Mansoor asked Hadhrat Imaam Maalik *(rahmatullahi alayh)*: "When making dua at the grave of Rasulullah ﷺ, should I face Nabi ﷺ or towards the Qiblah?" Imaam Maalik *(rahmatullahi alayh)* answered: "How can you possibly turn your face away from him when he is your medium *(waseelah)* as well as the *waseelah* of your father Hadhrat Aadam *(alayhis salaam)*. Turn your face to him and beg his intercession for you because Allah Ta'ala accepts his dua for you."

Conveying the salaams of others

After making salaam, now greet Nabi ﷺ for all those people who had asked you to give him their salaams. Say:

اَلسَّلَامُ عَلَيْكَ يَا رَسُوْلَ اللهِ مِنْ ..... يَسْتَشْفِعُ بِكَ اِلٰى رَبِّكَ

Salaam to you O Messenger of Allah from such and such a person who asks for your intercession."

*If you can't say it in Arabic then do so in your own language.

Greeting Hadhrat Abu Bakr and Hadhrat Umar (radiyallahu anhuma)

After greeting Rasulullah ﷺ, move one step to the right and make salaam to Hadhrat Abu Bakr ؓ. The body of Hadhrat Abu Bakr

At the Raudha Mubaarak of Rasulullah ﷺ

رَضِيَ اللَّهُ عَنْهُ is buried behind Rasulullah ﷺ and his head is in line with the shoulders of Rasulullah ﷺ. Thus Hadhrat Abu Bakr رَضِيَ اللَّهُ عَنْهُ will be about one step to the right of Rasulullah ﷺ.

Then take one more step to the right and make salaam to Hadhrat Umar رَضِيَ اللَّهُ عَنْهُ because Hadhrat Umar رَضِيَ اللَّهُ عَنْهُ is buried behind Hadhrat Abu Bakr رَضِيَ اللَّهُ عَنْهُ and his head is in line with the shoulders of Hadhrat Abu Bakr رَضِيَ اللَّهُ عَنْهُ.

If anyone had asked you to send salaams to Hadhrat Abu Bakr رَضِيَ اللَّهُ عَنْهُ and Hadhrat Umar رَضِيَ اللَّهُ عَنْهُ then do so and if you remember me, then give my salaams to them as well. May Allah reward you well for this!

Now stand in between Hadhrat Abu Bakr رَضِيَ اللَّهُ عَنْهُ and Hadhrat Umar رَضِيَ اللَّهُ عَنْهُ and make salaam to both of them together saying: *"Salaams to you both friends lying next to Rasulullah ﷺ who are his friends and helpers. May Allah Ta'ala reward you both well. We have come to you, begging your intercession with Rasulullah ﷺ so that he may intercede for us by Allah Ta'ala and ask Allah Ta'ala to cause us to stay as Muslims according to his sunnah and that he makes us on the Day of Qiyaamah from his special people and we are asking this dua also for all the Muslims."*

وَ صَاحِبَاكَ فَلَا اَنْسَاهُمَا اَبَدًا   مِنِّي السَّلَامُ عَلَيْكُمْ مَا جَرَي الْقَلَمِ

I can never forget your two companions, salaams from me upon you also as long as the pens will write

Return now to where you first stood facing Rasulullah ﷺ. Lift up your hands and thank Allah Ta'ala for all His favours. Recite Salawaat once more upon Rasulullah ﷺ and make dua to Allah Ta'ala through the *waseelah* (means) of Rasulullah ﷺ for yourself, your parents, your ustaads, your family and your friends and for all those who had asked you to make dua for them. Make dua for all the Muslim countries, for all the Muslims who are living and also for those who have died. If you remember then include me in your duas too.

Note: If it is not possible to make dua at the Raudha Mubaarak due to the large crowds, etc. one may move to some appropriate spot and engage in fervent dua to Allah Ta'ala.

General Advice

1. As far as possible, do not turn your back towards the Raudha Mubaarak, not even in salaah or out of salaah. In salaah, try at all times to stand in such a place where your front or your back is not towards the grave. Out of salaah there cannot be any possible reason why your back should ever be turned towards the grave.

2. When at any time you have to pass in front of the Raudha Mubaarak, stand quietly for a while and make salaam before carrying on. Some Ulama have said that even if you pass the masjid from the outside then you should still make salaam from there.

3. It is excellent to visit the Raudha Mubaarak many times. As long as the Haji is in Madinah Shareef, he should go again and again to the graveside to make salaam.

4. Whilst in Madinah Munawwarah, whenever you are inside the masjid, look towards the Raudha Mubaarak, where Rasulullah ﷺ is resting. When you are outside the Masjid then you should time and again look at the Green Dome above the grave. *Insha Allah*, you will get *sawaab* (reward) for doing this. When

looking at these two places, do so in silence and with due respect.

Virtues of visting the Raudha Mubaarak of Rasulullah ﷺ

Hadith No.1

Hadhrat Ibn Umar رضي الله عنه says that Rasulullah ﷺ said: "Whosoever visits my grave, my intercession becomes necessary for him." (i.e. I will definitely intercede with Allah Ta'ala on the day of Qiyaamah to forgive that person).

Hadith No.2

Hadhrat Ibn Umar رضي الله عنه says that Rasulullah ﷺ said: "Whosoever visits me after my death is like he who visited me during my life."

Hadith No.3

Rasulullah ﷺ said, "Whoever undertakes a journey, especially to visit my grave, will be my neighbour on the day of Qiyaamah and whoever lives in Madinah Munawwarah and patiently tolerates its hardships and difficulties, for him I will be a witness and intercessor on the day of Qiyaamah and, whoever dies in either of the Haramain

(Makkah or Madinah) will be raised on the day of Qiyaamah with those who have been granted safety."

Hadith No.4

Hadhrat Abu Hurayrah رَضِىَ اللهُ عَنْهُ reports that Rasulullah ﷺ said: "Whenever anyone makes salaam to me at my grave, Allah Ta'ala returns my soul to my body so that I reply to his greetings."

The meaning of returning the soul is that Allah Ta'ala gives Rasulullah ﷺ the ability to speak. After the passing away of Rasulullah ﷺ, his soul had already returned once and for all. Hence what actually now happens is that Nabi ﷺ returns the greetings by literally speaking.

Hadith No.5

It is reported that when a person stands at the grave of Rasulullah ﷺ and reads the aayah:

$$\text{اِنَّ اللهَ وَمَلٰئِكَتَهٗ يُصَلُّوْنَ عَلَى النَّبِيِّ يٰٓاَيُّهَا الَّذِيْنَ اٰمَنُوْا صَلُّوْا عَلَيْهِ وَ سَلِّمُوْا تَسْلِيْمًا}$$

and then says seventy times:

$$\text{صَلَّى اللهُ عَلَيْكَ يَا مُحَمَّدْ}$$

an angel says: 'May Allah's blessings be on you too, and then Allah fulfils his every need.'

In place of 'Yaa Muhammad', if we say 'Yaa Rasulallah' it would be better because we should not call Nabi ﷺ by his first name. I personally[1] feel that a visitor to the grave should at every visit recite seventy times with complete humility:

اَلصَّلٰوةُ وَالسَّلَامُ عَلَيْكَ يَا رَسُوْلَ اللهِ

This is excellent and better than reciting in a parrot fashion without understanding anything.

Hadith No.6

Hadhrat Abu Hurayrah رضي الله عنه reports that Rasulullah ﷺ said: "When a person stands at my grave reciting durood upon me, I hear it and whoever sends salaams upon me in any other place, his every need in this world and in the hereafter gets fulfilled and on the day of Qiyaamah I shall be his witness and intercessor."

An amazing incident regarding the Raudha Mubaarak

Sultan Nuruddin Zangi *(rahimahullah)* was a just ruler, and a very pious person who spent much of his time in salaah, meditation and zikrullah. He was a very saintly man whose nights were spent in Ibaadah. After performing Tahajjud Salaah one night, he went to sleep and in a dream

---

[1] *Refers to Hadhrat Shaikh Zakariyya (rahmatullahi alayh)*

he saw Rasulullah ﷺ who pointed towards two squint-eyed persons and said: "Protect me from these two."

The Sultan awoke in distress. He performed wudhu and read nafal salaah before going back to bed. He had hardly fallen asleep when he once again saw exactly the same dream. Once again he woke up, did as before and again fell asleep. He had hardly closed his eyes when he saw the same dream for the third time. This time he rose from his bed and realised that there was no time for sleep. Quickly, he called his wazir (a man called Jamaaluddin), who was also a very pious person. After having told him the story thus far, the wazir said: "Now there is no time to lose. Let us hasten to Madinah Munawwarah and let no one be informed of this dream."

Preparations were made very quickly and with twenty chosen men and fast camels loaded with goods they set forth. They travelled speedily by night and day. On the 16th day they arrived in Madinah Munawwarah from Egypt. They washed themselves outside Madinah Munawwarah and with due respect and humility came to the masjid to perform salaah in the Riyaadhul Jannah. There the Sultaan remained seated, deep in thought wondering what to do. Elsewhere, the wazir was making an announcement that the King had come for Ziyaarah and to distribute gifts to the people of Madinah Munawwarah. He also made arrangements for a huge feast to which all the people of Madinah Munawwarah were invited. All the people had come for the gifts. While these were distributed, the king stood by eagerly looking at the faces of all those who came forward. More and more people came but he did not see the two faces, which appeared in the dream.

When at last the king asked whether all the people of Madinah Munawwarah had come forward, it became known that there were two people who did not come. He was informed that there remained two pious people who had come from the west and usually distributed much charity. Neither did they take any gifts from anyone nor did they mix with the people. They appeared to be two very pious people.

The king summoned them to his presence and on seeing them, immediately recognised them. They were the ones shown to him by Rasulullah ﷺ in the dream. The king asked them: "Who are you?" They replied: "We are from the west. We have come to perform Haj and now have come here for Ziyaarah. We desire to stay here as neighbours of Rasulullah ﷺ and thus we are here." The king said: "I command you to tell me the truth."

Again they insisted on what they had said. The king inquired as to where they lived and was informed that they lived in a house just outside the masjid opposite the grave of Rasulullah ﷺ. Thereupon the king ordered them to be kept there in custody while he himself went to investigate. He began to inspect their house. There he found many goods, lots of wealth and books, etc. but the investigation brought forward nothing which could be connected with the dream. This left the king greatly troubled and worried. From all sides the people of Madinah Munawwarah came to intercede on their behalf, begging their release, saying: "These are two saintly and pious men. They fast by day and pray all night, saying their prayers in Riyaadhul Jannah, they visit Jannatul Baqee daily and every Saturday visit the Masjid of Quba. They never refuse any beggar and during the year of drought in Madinah Munawwarah, they were very generous to the people of Madinah."

When the king heard this, he was even more distressed, worried and amazed. He did not know what to do. Then a sudden thought came to him that he should lift up their musalla, which had been spread over the floor. Underneath was a hole which had been dug into the earth and which extended very near to the grave of Rasulullah ﷺ. When the people saw this they were speechless. Trembling in anger, the king started beating them excessively and said: "Speak the truth." At last they confessed that they were Christians, and a certain Christian king had given them much wealth and had promised them even more, if they disguised themselves as Hajis, proceeded to Madinah Munawwarah and removed the mubaarak body of Rasulullah ﷺ. Hence they came to Madinah. At night they dug a tunnel, took the sand in bags and spread it out at Baqee.

On hearing the true story, the king cried in gratitude. Allah Ta'ala and His Rasul ﷺ had chosen him for this great service. Thereafter he had them both killed. Then he had deep trenches dug all around the Raudha Mubaarak. It was so deep that the diggers had to dig till they reached the water level. He had the trenches filled with molten lead so that nobody could reach the body of Rasulullah ﷺ from underneath.

We will now end this section with the salaams presented by Hadhrat Mufti Mahmood Hasan Gangohi *(rahmatullahi alayh)* at the Raudha Mubaarak.

At the Raudha Mubaarak of Rasulullah ﷺ

سلام بدرگاہ خیر الانام صلی اللہ علیہ وآلہ وصحبہ وسلم

Salaam in the Court of the best of humanity ﷺ

Prepared by Faqeehul Ummat, Hadhrat Mufti Mahmood Hasan Gangohi

بڑھا پا ہے چلا ہوں سوئے یثرب

In my old age I am walking towards Yasrib

لرزتا لڑکھڑاتا سر جھکائے

Trembling, staggering with my head stooping low

گناہوں کا ہے سر پر بوجھ بھاری

My head is heavy with the burden of my sins

پریشاں ہوں اسے اب کون اٹھائے

I am worried, now who will carry this load of mine

کبھی آ جایا جو آنکھوں میں اندھیرا

Sometimes darkness veils my eyes all of a sudden

تو چکرا کر قدم بھی ڈگمگائے

Drowsiness renders my weak legs unstable

کبھی لاٹھی کبھی دیوار پکڑی

Sometimes a stick I hold and sometimes a wall

کبھی پھر بھی قدم جمنے نہ پائے

Then too my feet do not become steady at all

نہ بیٹا ہے نہ پوتا ہے نہ بھائی

I have no son, no grandson and no brother

کوئی گھر میں نہی جو ساتھ جائے

There's no one at home to go with me yonder

In the City of Rasulullah ﷺ

نہیں کچھ آرزو اب واپسی کی

I have no desire to return home

وہیں رکھے خدا واپس نہ لائے

May Allah keep me there never to return

مگر چلتا رہوں گا دھیرے دھیرے

But I would carry on walking step by step

دیا والا میری نیّا تراۓ

O Merciful One! Let my boat stay afloat

وہاں جا کر کہوں گا گڑ گڑا کر

I would go there and cry profusely and say

سلام اس پر جو گرتوں کو اٹھائے

Salaam upon Him who raises the fallen

سلام اُس پر جو سوتوں کو جگائے

Salaam upon Him who awakens the sleeping

سلام اس پر جو روتوں کو ہنسائے

Salaam upon Him who makes those who are crying laugh

سلام اس پر جو اجڑوں کو بسائے

Salaam upon Him who shelters the homeless

سلام اس پر جو بھوکوں کو کھلائے

Salaam upon Him who feeds the hungry

سلام اس پر جو پیاسوں کو پلائے

Salaam upon Him who quenches the thirsty

سلام اس پر جو گھڑیوں کو سجائے

Salaam upon Him who adorns the times

Riyaadhul Jannah

Next to the Raudha Mubaarak is a piece of land known as the Riyaadhul Jannah (garden of Jannah). This piece of land is actually a piece from Jannah which Allah Ta'ala sent down to this earth.

One morning after the Fajar Salaah, we walked towards the Riyaadhul Jannah and through the Grace of Allah Ta'ala, in the busy month of Ramadhaan, we managed to find some place comfortably in this garden of Jannah. No words can do justice in explaining the joy one experiences in sitting in this beautiful garden of Jannah. Really we were in the gardens of Jannah. Nabi-e-Kareem ﷺ has said that this place is Jannah and thus, this really is Jannah.

اور مدینے میں جنت موجود ہے ۔۔۔ یوں ہے جنت میں سب کچھ مدینہ نہیں

In Jannat one will find everything except Madinah, but in Madinah one will find Jannat exisiting there

The following dua began flowing from our lips,

"O Allah! You have taken us into Jannah and it is Your promise that when a Muslim enters Jannah, You will never take him out again. O Allah! We are now in Jannah right next to Rasulullah ﷺ and his two Noble Sahaabah (radiyallahu anhuma), O Allah, let it be that we are also blessed with such noble and great company in Jannatul Firdaus."

Al-hamdulillah! we sat there for approximately 45 minutes engaging in the recitation of durood shareef and making dua to Allah Ta'ala. Whilst sitting in this garden of Jannah, another thought crossed our minds. Once, Hadhrat Moulana Yunus Patel Saahib *(rahmatullahi alayh)* advised us that when sitting in the Riyaadhul Jannah, this is the closest a person can physically come to Rasulullah ﷺ. Hadhrat

Moulana *(rahmatullahi alayh)* advised that at such a time make dua to Allah Ta'ala,

"O Allah! You have given me the opportunity to come so close to Nabi ﷺ. However, spiritually I am very far from him. O my beloved Allah, just as you have brought me so close to my Nabi ﷺ physically, spiritually also make me close to him."

Brief explanation of the Riyaadhul Jannah

Hadhrat Abu Hurayrah رضى الله عنه reports that Rasulullah ﷺ said: "Between my house and my mimbar lies one of the gardens of Jannah and my mimbar stands upon my pond of water." [Bukhaari]

Shaikhul Hadith, Hadhrat Moulana Muhammad Zakariyya *(rahmatullahi alayh)*, has mentioned a beautiful explanation of Riyaadhul Jannah.

In the abovementioned Hadith, "between my house" means the room of Hadhrat Aa'ishah رضى الله عنها, wherein Rasulullah ﷺ is buried.

There are three explanations for this statement according to the learned Ulama.

1. Firstly, it may mean that the mercy of Allah Ta'ala descends on this area just as it descends continuously on the gardens of Jannah.
2. Secondly, it may mean that whoever performs ibaadah in this place shall receive one of the gardens of Jannah, which means that ibaadat (worship) in this spot is a means of acquiring a garden in Jannah.

3. Thirdly, it may mean that in actual fact this spot is a part of Jannah, placed here on earth, which shall, in its present form, once more be transported back to Jannah. Another Hadith points out: "A piece of Jannah the size of a bow is more virtuous than the earth and all that is in it."

Frame of mind in Madinah Munawwarah

One afternoon after the Asar Salaah, Hadhrat Mufti Saahib *(daamat barakaatuhu)* had given us a sterling piece of advice which should be engraved onto the heart of every person who visits the Haramain. He mentioned,

"When you come to the Haramain, come as a slave and not as a king. Come with your begging bowl in your hand. When you stand in front of the Raudha Mubaarak, stand like a beggar with your bowl in your hand hoping that something could be placed in it for you from the king. A beggar becomes oblivious of his surroundings. His focus and mind is on the king and his hope and desire is that he must be blessed with something. He also fears that he could be expelled from there at any time. A person who comes with this frame of mind does not then worry about what is happening in the Haram Shareef. He doesn't become a policeman, checking the behaviour and attitude of those that visit the Haram. He doesn't check who is playing with his cell phone and who is taking pictures, etc. His mind and focus is on his goal. A person who comes in with the temperament of a king will worry about what's happening around him. He then begins to complain about everything and everyone in the Haram Shareef whereas this is not the purpose of him coming here. In the Haramain one should practice on the verse, *'alaykum anfusakum'* (worry about yourselves).

Normally people can impress on others with their knowledge, piety, taqwa, akhlaaq and other qualities but what can you impress in front of Rasulullah ﷺ who is the fountainhead of ilm, piety, taqwa and akhlaaq. Stand with humility in front of Nabi ﷺ and hope that your bowl could be filled and you are sent back with respect."

Hadhrat Mufti Saahib *(daamat barakaatuhu)* did not like engaging in conversation in the Haram Shareef. He discouraged us from speaking, saying that in the Haram Shareef we should feel the presence of Rasulullah ﷺ.

CHAPTER Four

Masjidun Nabawi

When a person enters Madinah Munawwarah, from a distance he will notice the minarets of Masjidun Nabawi towering over the beautiful city. One's heart and mind becomes overawed with love for this beautiful Masjid and why should it not be so when this is the masjid of none other than the leader of mankind, Sayyidunah Rasulullah ﷺ himself.

This is the masjid where Rasulullah ﷺ performed his daily salaah. This is the masjid where Rasulullah ﷺ was the Imaam and his noble Sahaabah *(radiyallahu anhum)* were the *muqtadis* (followers). This is that masjid where Nabi ﷺ sat in I'tikaaf in the month of Ramadhaan, where he delivered his lectures, guided the Sahaabah *(radiyallahu anhum)* with his words of wisdom and prepared the Muslim armies to fight in the path of Allah Ta'ala. This is that masjid where Nabi ﷺ distributed the spoils of war to the poor and needy and this is where Nabi ﷺ lies resting till the day of Qiyaamah.

ذرا دیکھ لو مدینہ یہاں رحمتوں کے بادل یہ تلاوتوں کی محفل

یہ عبادتوں کی منزل کوئی رو رہا ہے پیارا، ہے درود لب پہ جاری

> *Just look at this beautiful city of Madinah, the clouds of mercy are hovering over. Look at the gatherings of tilaawat and the scene of Ibaadat. Someone is crying out of ecstacy whilst another is busy in the recitation of durood.*

Virtue of performing salaah in Masjidun Nabawi

It is mentioned in a Hadith narrated by Hadhrat Abu Hurayrah ﷺ that Rasulullah ﷺ said:

> *"One Salaah in this Masjid of mine is better than 1 000 salaah in any other Masjid besides Masjid-e-Haraam."* [Bukhaari Page 119]

Another Hadith recorded in Ibnu Majah says;

> *"One salaah in Masjidun Nabawi is equal to performing 50 000 salaah in any other place."* [Ibnu Majah #1413]

Building of Masjidun Nabawi

After migrating to Madinah Munawwarah, Nabi ﷺ was concerned about building a Masjid. There was a piece of land which was used for drying dates belonging to two orphans. Upon inquiry, Rasulullah ﷺ learnt that the owners of the land were two orphans by the name of Sahal and Suhail *(radiyallahu anhuma)*. Rasulullah

ﷺ called both of them to purchase this plot of land to erect a Masjid. Rasulullah ﷺ also spoke to their uncle, in whose care these orphans were, about purchasing the land. Both of them expressed a desire to donate the land to Rasulullah ﷺ without any rewards whatsoever saying that they hoped to reap the compensation from Allah Ta'ala alone. However, Rasulullah ﷺ declined to accept it without any remuneration. He paid them for the land.

Rasulullah ﷺ instructed Hadhrat Abu Bakr رضي الله عنه to pay for the plot of land. Hadhrat Abu Bakr رضي الله عنه paid ten Dinaars (gold coins) as a price for the land.

Thereafter Rasulullah ﷺ instructed the Sahaabah رضي الله عنهم to chop down the date palms and level the graves that were on the land. He then instructed them to produce unbaked bricks and he himself joined the Muhaajireen and Ansaar in the production of these bricks.

With the Sahaabah رضي الله عنهم, Rasulullah ﷺ would carry these bricks with great effort and chant:

اَللّٰهُمَّ لَاخَيْرَ اِلَّا خَيْرُ الْاٰخِرَةِ فَانْصُرِ الْاَنْصَارَ وَالْمُهَاجِرَةَ

"O Allah! There is no goodness except in the goodness of the hereafter. So assist the Muhaajireen and the Ansaar (who are aiming for the goodness of the hereafter only)."

The Sahaabah رضي الله عنهم, in the meantime were chanting:

لَئِنْ قَعَدْنَا وَالنَّبِيُّ يَعْمَلُ لَذَاكَ مِنَ الْعَمَلِ الْمُضَلِّلِ

"If we sit down whilst Nabi ﷺ toils, this action of ours (this sitting) would be extremely detestable."

Talq bin Ali ﷺ narrates: "Rasulullah ﷺ instructed me to mix the mortar. Taking a shovel in hand, I got up to mix the mortar." He says: "I asked, O Rasulullah ﷺ! Should I not carry the bricks as well?" Rasulullah ﷺ replied: "No, you should rather stick to mixing mortar, as you are more skilled in this regard."

This Masjid was unique in its simplicity. The walls were constructed of unbaked bricks. The pillars were hewn from the trunks of date palms. The roof was fabricated from the leaves and branches of date palms. Whenever it rained, water would seep through into the Masjid. Later on, the roof was plastered with mortar. It was a hundred cubits long and approximately a hundred cubits wide (about 45 meters). The foundations were about three cubits deep (1.3 meters). The height was slightly higher than the height of an average man. The Qiblah wall was facing Baitul-Muqaddas (in Jerusalem). Three doors were erected in the Masjid structure. One door was placed on the side where the Qiblah is today. The second door was positioned on the western wall and is today referred to as Baabur-Rahmah. The third door was the door frequently used by Rasulullah ﷺ and is today referred to as Baabu Jibraa'eel.

After about sixteen or seventeen months, when the Qiblah direction was moved from Baitul-Muqaddas to the K'abah for the performance of Salaah, the door at the back (previously the front) of the Masjid was sealed off and another door was erected directly opposite it.

Masjid-e-Nabawi underwent contruction twice (during the time of Rasulullah ﷺ). The first time it was erected was when Rasulullah ﷺ migrated and lived at the residence of Hadhrat Abu Ayyub Ansaari *(radiyallahu anhu)*. The second time it was renovated in the year 7 A.H. after the battle of Khaybar, when the Masjid fell into disrepair.

In the initial construction, the length and the breadth of the Masjid was under a hundred cubits (45 meters) whilst it was extended to just over a hundred cubits in the subsequent construction.

When Rasulullah ﷺ planned to extend the Masjid, he approached the Ansaari owner of the adjoining plot of land and said: "Sell us this land in exchange of a palace in Jannah." The Ansaari, due to his poverty and excessive dependants, was unable to offer the land for free. This is why Hadhrat 'Usmaan رضي الله عنه purchased this plot in exchange of 10 000 Dirhams from this Ansaari. Appearing before Rasulullah ﷺ, he submitted: "O Rasulullah ﷺ! The plot of land you wished to purchase from the Ansaari in exchange of a palace in Jannah, please purchase it from me (in exchange of that palace)." Rasulullah ﷺ purchased this plot from Hadhrat 'Usmaan رضي الله عنه in exchange of a palace in Jannah and incorporated this plot of land into the Masjid. Rasulullah ﷺ placed the first brick with his own blessed hand and, as per his instructions, the next brick was placed by Hadhrat Abu Bakr رضي الله عنه, then by Hadhrat 'Umar رضي الله عنه, followed by Hadhrat 'Usmaan رضي الله عنه and then by Hadhrat Ali رضي الله عنه.

Hadhrat Abu Hurayrah رضي الله عنه, who embraced Islam in the 7th year of Hijrah, also joined them in this reconstruction of the Masjid. Hadhrat Abu Hurayrah رضي الله عنه himself narrates: "Rasulullah ﷺ himself carried the heavy stones with the Sahaabah رضي الله عنهم in the reconstruction of the Masjid. He was supporting the stones onto his chest. I thought that he was holding them close to his chest because of their substantial weight. I submitted: 'O Rasulullah! Hand them over to me. I will carry them.' Rasulullah ﷺ replied: 'Take another lot of stones, Abu Hurayrah. There is no life but the life of the hereafter.'"

Pillars in Masjidun Nabawi

Mullah Ali Qaari *(rahmatullahi alayh)* writes: "Those pillars of the Masjid, which are of special virtue, should indeed be visited by the visitor to Madinah Munawwarah. There he should keep himself busy with voluntary (nafal) salaah and dua. This applies especially to that portion of the Masjid which used to be the Masjid during the time of Rasulullah ﷺ (before its extension). The pillars in this area are extremely blessed. According to Imaam Bukhaari *(rahmatullahi alayh)*, the Sahaabah *(radiyallahu anhum)* of Rasulullah ﷺ used to offer much salaah at these pillars. They are eight in number."

1. Ustuwaana-e-Hannanah

Ustuwaan-e-Hannanah is also known as the weeping pillar. This is the most blessed of all the pillars for this was the place of salaah for Rasulullah ﷺ. There was a date trunk on this spot. Before the mimbar was built, Rasulullah ﷺ used to lean on it while delivering the khutbah (sermon). When the mimbar was built, Rasulullah ﷺ began using the mimbar for the khutbah. It so happened that when this change took place, the tree wept so bitterly that the whole Masjid echoed and those in the Masjid began weeping. Rasulullah ﷺ went to the tree, placed his mubaarak hand on it and the crying stopped. Rasulullah ﷺ then said: "The tree cries because the zikr of Allah Ta'ala was heard near it, and now that the mimbar is built, it has been deprived of this zikr. Therefore it weeps. If I did not place my hand on it, it would have cried till the day of Qiyaamah." Afterwards the tree dried up and was buried.

2. Ustuwaana-e-Aa'ishah رَضِيَ اللهُ عَنْهَا

Hadhrat Aa'ishah رَضِيَ اللهُ عَنْهَا reports that Rasulullah صَلَّى اللهُ عَلَيْهِ وَسَلَّمَ said: "In this Masjid there is one such spot that if people knew how blessed it is, they would flock towards it in such numbers, that to perform salaah there they would have had to cast lots." People asked her to point out the exact spot which she refused to do. Later on, at the persistence of Abdullah Ibn Zubair رَضِيَ اللهُ عَنْهُ, she pointed out this spot. Hence it is called Ustuwaan-e-Aa'ishah, because the Hadith is reported by her and the exact spot was shown by her. Hadhrat Abu Bakr رَضِيَ اللهُ عَنْهُ and Hadhrat Umar رَضِيَ اللهُ عَنْهُ used to perform salaah here very often.

3. Ustuwaana-e-Taubah

This pillar is also known as Ustuwaan-e-Abu Lubabah. Abu Lubabah رَضِيَ اللهُ عَنْهُ was one of the famous Sahaabah. During the battle against the Banu Quraizah, whilst the Muslims had laid a siege over them, he became impatient and wanted to throw down his arms. Before he accepted Islam, he had many dealings with the Jews of Banu Quraizah. Now after the Jews had deceived the Muslims, the Jews called him during the siege to find out from him what Rasulullah صَلَّى اللهُ عَلَيْهِ وَسَلَّمَ intended to do to them for their betrayal. When he reached them, they all began wailing and crying. He was affected by this and indicated towards his throat suggesting that they would be killed. After having done that he became so saddened at this mistake that he could not rest. He thereupon came to the Masjid and here at this spot where a date tree used to stand, he bound himself to the trunk saying: "As long as my repentance is not accepted by Allah Ta'ala, I shall not untie myself from this tree. Rasulullah صَلَّى اللهُ عَلَيْهِ وَسَلَّمَ himself must untie me." When Rasulullah

ﷺ heard this he said: "If he had come to me I would have begged for forgiveness on his behalf. Now he has acted on his own initiative, so how can I untie him until such a time that his repentance has been accepted."

For many days he remained tied there, except for salaah and for the call of nature for which his wife and daughter used to untie him and then again tie him to the tree. He remained without food or drink as a result of which his sight and hearing were affected. After a few days, one morning, whilst Rasulullah ﷺ was performing Tahajjud Salaah in the house of Umm-e-Salama *(radiyallahu anha)*, he received the good news that his taubah had been accepted. The Sahaabah *(radiyallahu anhum)* conveyed the news to him, and wanted to untie him but he refused, saying: "As long as Nabi ﷺ does not untie me with his blessed hands, I shall not allow anyone else to do so." When Rasulullah ﷺ entered the masjid for Fajar Salaah he untied him. This spot is very near the one at which Rasulullah ﷺ sat for I'tikaaf, and most of the poor and needy ones used to be seated there. Rasulullah ﷺ very often used to remain there with them after Fajar till the sun rose.

4. Ustuwaana-e-Sareer

Sareer means sleeping place. It is reported that Rasulullah ﷺ used to also make I'tikaaf here, and used to sleep here whilst in I'tikaaf. A platform of wood used to be put here for him to sleep on.

5. Ustuwaana-e-Ali رَضِىَ اللّٰهُ عَنْهُ

This used to be the place where some of the Sahaabah (radiyallahu anhum) used to sit when keeping watch or acting as gate keepers. Hadhrat Ali رَضِىَ اللّٰهُ عَنْهُ used to be the one who mostly sat here and kept watch, therefore it is often called Ustuwaan-e-Ali رَضِىَ اللّٰهُ عَنْهُ.

6. Ustuwaana-e-Wufood

Wufood means delegations. Whenever delegations arrived to meet Rasulullah ﷺ on behalf of their tribes, they sat here. He used to converse with them and teach them Deen at this spot.

7. Ustuwaana-e-Tahajjud

It is reported that this was the spot where late at night a carpet was spread for Rasulullah ﷺ to perform Tahajjud Salaah, after all the people had left. According to some reports, this was also the place where for three nights Rasulullah ﷺ performed his Taraaweeh Salaah. A very large group of Sahaabah gathered to follow him at this spot.

8. Ustuwaana-e-Jibra'eel

This was the usual place where Jibraeel (alayhis salaam) would enter to visit Rasulullah ﷺ. Today it cannot be seen as it lies inside the Hujra (room) of Rasulullah ﷺ.

These are eight special spots mentioned by the Ulama. However, which part of Masjid-e-Nabawi is there where the mubaarak feet of Rasulullah

ﷺ did not touch or where he and the Sahaabah (*radiyallahu anhum*) did not perform their salaah? In fact which part of Madinah Munawwarah is there where these saintly souls did not tread? Every step taken in Madinah Munawwarah is a step on 'blessed ground'. May Allah Ta'ala help us all to benefit from the blessings of this holy and sacred place. *Aameen.*

Suffah and As-haabus Suffah

A Suffah is actually a ledge or a covered veranda. The weak and destitute Muslims who dedicated their lives to learning Deen from Nabi ﷺ would remain at this spot. People would refer to this group as As-haabus Suffah. It was as though this was the Khaanqah of Rasulullah ﷺ.

The As-haabus Suffah were a group of people who were neither interested in trade nor was farming of any concern to them. These people had dedicated their sight to behold Rasulullah ﷺ and their ears to listen to his sacred words. They had totally surrendered themselves to the companionship of Rasulullah ﷺ.

Hadhrat Abu Hurayrah ؓ who was one of the more famous companions of the Suffah relates: "I was also from amongst the As-haabus-Suffah. Every evening we would present ourselves before Rasulullah ﷺ. He would distribute us in ones or twos amongst the more affluent Sahaabah ؓ. He would then himself take those who were left. After meals, we would all sleep in the Masjid.

Hadhrat Abu Hurayrah ؓ narrates: "I have observed seventy As-haabus Suffah who did not even possess a single sheet to cover themselves. They merely owned a sheet or a blanket to cover the lower portion of their bodies. Even these blankets were so short that they would barely reach half their calves or their ankles and they would hold it close to their bodies lest their Satar became exposed."

Waasilah bin Asq'a ﷺ relates: "I was also one of the members of As-haabus Suffah. None of us even had a complete set of clothing. Due to excessive perspiration, our bodies were covered with grime and dust."

Hadhrat Abu Hurayrah ﷺ relates: "I swear by that Being besides whom there is no other god that quite often, overwhelmed with hunger, I would lay my chest and stomach onto the ground (so that the moisture and coolness of the ground may alleviate the heat of my hunger to some extent). Occasionally I would fasten a stone to my stomach merely to keep my back straight.

One day I seated myself at one of the main thoroughfares when Hadhrat Abu Bakr ﷺ happened to pass by. I asked him to explain a certain aayat of the Qur-aan to me but my actual intention was that he might catch sight of my pitiful condition and take me along for a meal. However, Hadhrat Abu Bakr ﷺ went away (without realizing my intention).

A little later Hadhrat 'Umar ﷺ happened to pass by. In a like manner, on the pretext of explaining a Qur-aanic aayat to me I intercepted him. However he too went on his way. A little while later Abul-Qaasim ﷺ (whom Allah Ta'ala sent as a Qaasim – distributor – of blessings) happened to pass by the same way. The moment his gaze fell on me, he realised my intentions. Smiling at me, he said: 'O Abu Hirr!' 'I am at your service, O Rasulullah ﷺ!' I replied, 'Come along with me' he said. I went along with him to his house. As he entered his home, he found a bowl of milk there. When he enquired about it, his family replied: 'So and so sent it as a gift to you.' Looking towards me, he asked me to call the As-haabus Suffah."

Hadhrat Abu Hurayrah ﷺ relates: "The As-haabus Suffah were the guests of Islam. They neither had a place to live nor were they in possession of any wealth. Whenever any charity came to Rasulullah ﷺ, he would send it over to them without partaking of any part of it (because Sadaqah was Haraam for him). Whenever he received a gift, he would partake of it and include the As-haabus Suffah in it as well. Now when he asked me to call the As-haabus Suffah, I found it a bit diffficult. I thought to myself, how would this one bowl of milk suffice for all the As-haabus Suffah? I am most eligible to drink this milk. At least I would be able to regain some of my strength. Furthermore, after the arrival of the As-haabus Suffah, I myself would be instructed to serve the milk to them. I do not think that there would be any leftover for me. Nevertheless, there was no getting away from obeying Allah and His Rasool ﷺ.

I called the As-haabus Suffah and as per Rasulullah's ﷺ instructions, I served them one by one. When all of them drank to their full, Rasulullah ﷺ smiled at me and said: 'Only you and I are left now.' I said: 'That is correct, O Rasulullah (ﷺ)' Rasulullah ﷺ asked me to start drinking. As I was drinking, he repeatedly asked me to drink saying: 'Drink more! Drink more!' until such time that I was completely full and cried out: 'By that Being Who has sent you with the truth! I do not have space for any more.' Taking the bowl from my hand, Rasulullah ﷺ recited some praises of Allah, said *Bismillah* and drank up whatever remained in the bowl."

Abdur-Rahmaan bin Abi Bakr ﷺ relates: "The As-haabus Suffah were extremely destitute. Rasulullah ﷺ would distribute them amongst the Sahaabah ﷺ saying: "He who has food for two should take a third person with him and he who has food for three should take a fourth person with him," and so forth.

Muhammad bin Seereen *(rahmatullahi alayh)* says: "Towards the evening, Rasulullah ﷺ would distribute the As-haabus Suffah amongst his Sahaabah ؓ. Some of them would take two whilst others would take three of them home. S'ad bin 'Ubaadah ؓ would sometimes take up to eighty people home with him for meals." A string was tied between two pillars of the Masjid. The Ansaar who had date orchards would hang up a few clusters of dates for the As-haabus Suffah. They would strike the dates with a stick and eat as they fell to the ground. Hadhrat Mu'aaz bin Jabal ؓ was in charge of this.

Once, Rasulullah ﷺ came out from his house and entered the Masjid carrying a staff when his gaze fell onto a spoilt cluster of dates suspended in the Masjid. He commented: "If the donor wished, he could have brought a better bunch of dates."

According to another Hadith, Rasulullah ﷺ instructed every date palm owner to bring a bunch of dates and hang it up in the Masjid for the destitute.

Jaabir bin Abdullah ؓ narrates that Rasulullah ﷺ said: "From every ten clusters of dates, one cluster should be placed in the Masjid for the destitute."

Fudaalah bin 'Ubaid ؓ narrates: "Quite often, overwhelmed with severe hunger, the As-haabus Suffah would fall down unconscious whilst performing Salaah. If a villager or Bedouin had to lay eyes on them, he would think of them to have lost their senses or regard them as lunatics. Rasulullah ﷺ would come to them and console them thus:

"If only you knew what awaits you by Allah, you would wish for an increase in this poverty and need."

CHAPTER Five

Virtues of Madinah Munawwarah

"There is no piece of land that is more beloved to me that I be buried therein, than Madinah Munawwarah" [Hadith] [1]

This Hadith is sufficient to explain the virtue of Madinah Shareef. Every part of this city is so unique. Naturally it has a great attraction. Every part of this city is lit up with divine light and why should it not be so when it is the city of Rasulullah ﷺ. Munawwarah means 'lit up' with divine light.

In order to appreciate a place, one has to first understand its virtues. Below are some of the virtues of Madinah Munawwarah as

---

[1] *Muatta Imaam Maalik. Page 478*

mentioned by Hadhrat Shaikh Zakariyya *(rahmatullahi alayh)* in his book Fazaail-e-Haj:

The city of Madinah Munawwarah deserves great honour and respect. It is a city which was once filled with divine revelations from Allah Ta'ala. Many parts of the Qur-aan Shareef were revealed here. On numerous occasions, Jibraeel *(alayhis salaam)*, Meekaaeel *(alayhis salaam)* and other respected angels visited the earth. In all corners the praises of Allah Ta'ala and His Nabi ﷺ were heard. The dust and the earth became honoured through the presence of Rasulullah ﷺ, at those places where he stayed and rested. Such a place is indeed worthy of respect where the commands of Allah Ta'ala and the practices of His Rasul ﷺ were announced and to this day the numerous relics of spiritual blessings and righteousness can be seen. Such places need to be honoured, their fragrance inhaled and their walls kissed in honour.

Hadith No. 1 – The names of Madinah Munawwarah

Jaabir ibn Samurah ؓ says: "I heard Rasulullah ﷺ say: 'Verily Allah Ta'ala named Madinah, Taabah (meaning the good one) or Tayyibah (the pure one).'" [Muslim]

Taabah and Tayyibah mean clean, pure, excellent, thereby meaning that it is free of all the evils of shirk. It may also mean that the climate around the city is completely favourable for those with the correct nature and temperament. It also means that the people of the city are righteous and pious. These are some of the reasons mentioned for naming the city Taabah.

Madinah has more than a thousand names but five names are more famous viz. Madinah, Taabah, Tayyibah, Daar and Yasrib. In the days of ignorance it used to be called Yasrib. However, Rasulullah ﷺ did not approve of this name. The most obvious reason for Rasulullah's ﷺ dislike is that the name Yasrib means blame and sadness. It was a habit of Rasulullah ﷺ to change all those names which were unsuitable or disapproved.

Hadith No. 2 – Madinah casts off all evil

Hadhrat Abu Hurayrah رضي الله عنه reports that Rasulullah ﷺ said: "I have been commanded to take up residence in such a village that consumes all villages. They call it Yasrib and its name is Madinah. She (Madinah) casts off the evil ones as dirt is removed when iron is melted."

[Bukhaari and Muslim]

This Hadith draws our attention to many points. Firstly it mentions that Rasulullah ﷺ was commanded to take up residence in Madinah Munawwarah. This makes it clear that Rasulullah ﷺ did not settle there of his own desire, but that it was Allah Ta'ala's wish that he does so. Hadhrat Umar رضي الله عنه reports that Allah Ta'ala, the Glorious selected Madinah Munawwarah for His Nabi ﷺ.

Further, Rasulullah ﷺ said: "The place of my migration has been shown to me. It is a saline land situated between rocky lands. It shall be either Hajr or Madinah."

In another Hadith it is reported that Hadhrat Abu Bakr رضي الله عنه wanted permission to migrate to Madinah Munawwarah. Rasulullah ﷺ told him: "Wait a while. Soon permission will be granted to me as well." It is also reported that in those days Hadhrat Abu Bakr رضي الله عنه saw in a dream that the moon descended from the heavens onto Makkah whereby the whole city became bright. Thereafter the moon ascended and this time descended in Madinah Munawwarah, brightening the whole city. Then it entered the house of Hadhrat Aa'ishah رضي الله عنها where the ground split open and the moon disappeared therein. Hadhrat Abu Bakr رضي الله عنه who knew the meaning of dreams, knew that it referred to Rasulullah ﷺ travelling from Makkah Mukarramah to Madinah Munawwarah where he would pass away to be buried inside the room of Hadhrat Aa'ishah رضي الله عنها.

It is also mentioned in this Hadith that "the city casts off evil people in a similar manner as molten metal casts off dirt." Some say it means Islam destroying all idolatry beliefs in the early years of Islam. In another Hadith there is a story of a bedouin who lived in Madinah Munawwarah. Once he was troubled by a very high fever, as a result of which he intended leaving Madinah Munawwarah. He came to Rasulullah ﷺ and begged his permission to break his oath of allegiance, thereby allowing him to depart from Madinah Munawwarah. Rasulullah ﷺ did not grant him permission. Thereafter he repeatedly came with the same request, which Rasulullah ﷺ always turned down. However, without permission he departed whereupon Rasulullah ﷺ said: "Like fire that casts off dirt from iron that is melted, so also does Madinah cast away evil people, and purifies the righteous."

Some Ulama state that this will take place during the final days. In the time of Dajjaal, all evil ones will depart from Madinah Munawwarah.

According to the Hadith, "Qiyaamah shall not take place until such a time that all evil ones have departed from Madinah." Imaam Bukhaari *(rahmatullahi alayh)* relates a Hadith: "Dajjaal shall pass through every city except Madinah Munawwarah and Makkah Mukarramah. Here he shall not enter. The angels shall protect these two cities. During the final days, three earthquakes shall shake the city whereby every non-believer and evil person shall depart."

The fifth point mentioned in this Hadith is the virtue of Madinah Munawwarah over all other cities. It is an agreed fact that Madinah Munawwarah is above all cities in virtue except Makkah Mukarramah. It is agreed among all the Ulama that the portion of the earth attached to the mubaarak body of Rasulullah ﷺ and the area that surrounds it is the most virtuous in rank, and noblest of all the earth (even nobler than the Ka'bah Shareef).

Qadhi Iyaadh *(rahmatullahi alayh)* says it is even higher in rank than the Throne of Allah Ta'ala. The Ulama have said that every person was originally created from the sand wherein he is buried. Hence we conclude that the body of Rasulullah ﷺ was originally created from the earth wherein he now lies and as such, he being the most virtuous, lies buried in the most virtuous earth. The mubaarak body of Rasulullah ﷺ in Madinah Munawwarah brings many mercies and blessings continuously upon this city.

Rasulullah ﷺ is reported to have said: "There is no land which is more beloved in my sight and wherein I would prefer my grave to be than Madinah."

Hadith No. 3 – Residency in Madinah Munawwarah

Hadhrat Sa'ad ؓ reports that Rasulullah ﷺ said: "I declare haraam that area lying between the rocky lands on both sides of Madinah. Its vegetation should not be cut down and its animals should not be hunted."

Rasulullah ﷺ also said: "For a Muslim, Madinah is the best place. If only they could understand its virtue fully, they would never leave it, and whoever departs from Madinah, having become bored with it, Allah Ta'ala will send someone better to replace him. And whoever bears patiently the hardships of living in Madinah Munawwarah, for him shall I be an intercessor (or witness) on the day of Qiyaamah." [Muslim]

In this Hadith mention is made of a Haram (sanctuary / place of safety) in Madinah Munawwarah. The area declared a Haram here is the sandy area of Madinah lying between the rocky areas bordering the city on two sides. Hadhrat Ali رضي الله عنه reports that Rasulullah ﷺ said: "I declare a Haram the area between Mount Ayr and Saur." Mount Saur is a low mountain near Mount Uhud. Haram here means that this area is to be honoured and respected, that no animals be hunted, nor any vegetation destroyed as is the case with the Haram in Makkah.

Residency

The second point in this Hadith deals with residence in Madinah Munawwarah. Rasulullah ﷺ said, "Yemen shall be conquered. Then some people will move there in order to investigate conditions. Then they with their families and all who follow them will go to Yemen. Yet at that time Madinah Munawwarah shall be better for them, if only they knew of Madinah's blessings.

Syria will be conquered. Some people on hearing of conditions there will move there with their families and followers. Yet at that time too Madinah Munawwarah will be better for them, if only they knew.

Iraq shall be conquered. Some people learning of conditions there will move in that direction with their families and followers. Yet Madinah Munawwarah would be better for them, if they only knew."

Ibn Hajar *(rahmatullahi alayh)* says that this prophecy turned out to be true and these areas were conquered in the exact order as mentioned in the Hadith.

Abu Usaid ﷺ reports: "When Hadhrat Hamzah ﷺ, the uncle of Rasulullah ﷺ became shaheed, we were present with Rasulullah ﷺ at his grave. The body of Hadhrat Hamzah ﷺ was shrouded in a cloth of insufficient length, which could not cover the body fully. When it was pulled over his face, his feet were uncovered and when his feet were covered, his face became uncovered. Thereupon, Rasulullah ﷺ commanded that his face be covered and leaves be used to cover his feet in the grave. The Sahaabah *(radiyallahu anhum)* (noting this poverty) shed tears and wept. Then Rasulullah ﷺ said: "A time shall come over my people, when, to foreign lands they shall proceed, where, in abundance they shall find food and drink, and animals to ride on. From there shall they then write to their relatives and dependants and ask, 'Why are you still chained to the drought-stricken desert lands of Hejaz? Come and live here.' Yet, Madinah Munawwarah will be better for them, if only they knew..." *[Targheeb]*

Imaam Muslim *(rahmatullahi alayh)* reports: "Soon on seeing new towns, their wealth and produce, people will call their near relatives; 'Come to settle here. Here is a land of abundance,' but Madinah Munawwarah will be better for them, O! if only they would realise it."

What Rasulullah ﷺ said is indeed true, because in spite of all the worldly wealth other places may have, Madinah Munawwarah is still superior in blessings to those wealthy places, and in the good fortune of having the presence of Rasulullah ﷺ. Furthermore, the love for Islam found in Madinah Munawwarah is not experienced in any other place and the value of this alone is countless.

Hadhrat Moulana Qaasim Nanotwi *(rahmatullahi alayh)* used to say the following poetry;

جیوں تو ساتھ سگانِ حرم کے تیرے پھروں   مروں تو کھائیں مدینے کے مجھ کو مُور ومار

I hope that among the dogs of your sacred Haram I shall roam, till the end of my days, and that I be eaten by the ants and snakes of Madinah

اُڑا کے باد مری مشتِ خاک کو پس مرگ   کرے حضور کے روضہ کے آ پاس نثار

And I hope that on having turned to dust at death, the wind shall spread my dust over the Rowdha Mubarak.

Patiently bearing the difficulties in Madinah

The next topic discussed in the Hadith concerns the one who patiently bears the difficulties of life in Madinah Munawwarah. Rasulullah ﷺ will act as an intercessor or a witness for such a person.

Once, while Madinah Munawwarah was under attack in the battle of Harrah and the city was surrounded by the enemy, the people of Madinah Munawwarah experienced great difficulty. A man came to Hadhrat Abu Sa'eed Khudhri ؓ complaining of hardship and difficulty and seeking advice about moving out of Madinah Munawwarah. Hadhrat Abu Sa'eed ؓ replied: "Never! I shall never give you such advice for I have personally heard Rasulullah ﷺ saying; 'Whoever bears patiently the trials and hardships of Madinah Munawwarah, and suffers patiently the pangs of hunger, for him I shall be an intercessor on the day of Qiyaamah.'"

Hadith No. 4 – Muslims flocking to Madinah Shareef

Hadhrat Abu Hurayrah ﺭﺿﻲ ﺍﻟﻠﻪ ﻋﻨﻪ reports that Rasulullah ﺻﻠﻰ ﺍﻟﻠﻪ ﻋﻠﻴﻪ ﻭﺳﻠﻢ said: *"Imaan shall flow back to Madinah, as a snake returns to its hole."*
[Bukhaari]

Some of the Ulama explain that this refers to the early days of Islam during Rasulullah's ﺻﻠﻰ ﺍﻟﻠﻪ ﻋﻠﻴﻪ ﻭﺳﻠﻢ lifetime and the time of the first four Khulafaa and the time of the Sahaabah. All those who had any enthusiasm for Imaan in their hearts flocked to Madinah Munawwarah to visit Rasulullah ﺻﻠﻰ ﺍﻟﻠﻪ ﻋﻠﻴﻪ ﻭﺳﻠﻢ, and to acquire the knowledge of Deen.

According to some Ulama it refers to all times to come when people will flock to Madinah Munawwarah to visit the grave of Rasulullah ﺻﻠﻰ ﺍﻟﻠﻪ ﻋﻠﻴﻪ ﻭﺳﻠﻢ and perform salaah in Masjid-e-Nabawi, and visit the sacred sites, etc.

Other Ulama however say that this refers to the latter days when from all over the world Deen will come back to Madinah Munawwarah. The view of these is supported by a Hadith reported in Tirmizi by Hadhrat Abu Hurayrah ﺭﺿﻲ ﺍﻟﻠﻪ ﻋﻨﻪ which says: *"Of the cities of Islam, the one that shall be destroyed last near the time of Qiyaamah will be Madinah."* (Mishkaat)

Hadith No. 5 – The Blessings of Madinah

Hadhrat Anas ﺭﺿﻲ ﺍﻟﻠﻪ ﻋﻨﻪ says that Nabi ﺻﻠﻰ ﺍﻟﻠﻪ ﻋﻠﻴﻪ ﻭﺳﻠﻢ once made dua, *"O Allah, grant to Madinah double the blessings that You have granted to Makkah."* [Bukhaari and Muslim]

Hadhrat Abu Hurayrah ﷺ says that it used to be the habit of the Sahaabah *(radiyallahu anhum)* that whenever the first fruits of the season were picked, they used to place it before Rasulullah ﷺ, who then used to take it and make dua thus,

اَللّٰهُمَّ بَارِكْ لَنَا فِيْ ثَمَرِنَا وَبَارِكْ لَنَا فِيْ مَدِيْنَتِنَا وَبَارِكْ لَنَا فِيْ صَاعِنَا وَبَارِكْ لَنَا فِيْ مُدِّنَا

> "O Allah, grant us blessings in our fruits, and bless us in this town of ours, and bless us in our 'Saa' and in our 'Mudd' (both are measures),"

> "O Allah, Ibrahim (alayhis salaam) was Your servant, Your friend and Your Nabi. I am also Your servant and Your Nabi. As Ibrahim (alayhis salaam) made dua for blessings in Makkah, so do I make dua for double blessings in Madinah."

Thereafter Rasulullah ﷺ gave the fruit to a young child. In this Hadith reference is made to Hadhrat Ibrahim's *(alayhis salaam)* dua which is in the Qur-aan:

فَاجْعَلْ اَفْئِدَةً مِّنَ النَّاسِ تَهْوِىٓ اِلَيْهِمْ وَارْزُقْهُمْ مِّنَ الثَّمَرٰتِ لَعَلَّهُمْ يَشْكُرُوْنَ

> "So fill the hearts of the people with love towards them and feed them with fruits so that they may show gratitude."

In another Hadith, Hadhrat Ibrahim's *(alayhis salaam)* desire in his dua was for blessings in the meat and water of Makkah Mukarramah. It is said that Rasulullah's ﷺ dua was for similar blessings.

Note that 'Saa' and 'Mudd' are two measures whereby grain like wheat etc., were measured. The dua for blessings in these is in fact a dua for blessings in sustenance from Allah Ta'ala. According to our pious Ulama, this dua of Rasulullah ﷺ was definitely answered as experience has shown, so much so that the amount of food which is sufficient for those in and around Madinah Munawwarah, the same amount of food will not suffice for any other place. Whoever lives in Madinah Munawwarah can testify to having experienced this.

Hadith No. 6 – Deceiving or hurting the people of Madinah

Hadhrat Sa'ad ﷺ reports that Rasulullah ﷺ said: "Whoever plans to deceive the people of Madinah shall become destroyed as salt is dissolved in water." [Bukhaari and Muslim]

According to a Hadith in Muslim Shareef, Rasulullah ﷺ said: "Whoever desires to commit any crime against the people of Madinah, Allah Ta'ala shall destroy him as fire melts metal or as salt dissolves in water."

Hadhrat Jaabir ﷺ once said: "May that person become destroyed who threatens our Rasulullah ﷺ." His son replied: "How can that be, since Rasulullah ﷺ has passed away? How can anyone threaten him?" Jaabir ﷺ replied: "Verily I heard Nabi ﷺ say: 'Whoever threatens the people of Madinah Munawwarah, does indeed threaten this heart of mine.'"

In another Hadith we read: "Whoever frightens the people of Madinah Shareef, Allah Ta'ala shall frighten him." Ubaadah ﷺ reports that Rasulullah ﷺ said: "O Allah, whenever anyone persecutes or frightens the people of Madinah Shareef, You then frighten him. May the curse of Allah Ta'ala and His angels and the whole world descend upon him. Neither shall his fardh acts nor his nafal acts be accepted."

Zaid bin Aslam رَضِيَ اللّٰهُ عَنْهُ also reports that Rasulullah ﷺ made this dua against those who desire evil against the people of Madinah.

Note: These words are indeed frightening and should be taken seriously, especially by those who visit Madinah Munawwarah. They should be very careful that they do not hurt the people, injure their feelings or deceive them in their dealings. To deal with them dishonestly means to expose oneself to destruction. When dealing with them, try to deal with them with the utmost honesty.

Hadith No. 7 – Forty Salaah in Masjidun Nabawi

Hadhrat Anas رَضِيَ اللّٰهُ عَنْهُ reports that Rasulullah ﷺ said, "Whoever performs forty salaah in my Masjid, not missing one salaah in the Masjid, for him is freedom from the fire of Jahannam, and freedom from punishment and he shall remain free of hypocrisy." [Ahmad and Tabraani]

This is indeed a great reward which is easy for the visitor to Madinah Munawwarah to obtain. They should stay in Madinah Munawwarah for at least eight days. In this manner they will get their forty salaah in Masjidun Nabawi. They should definitely try their utmost not to miss one salaah in between. If they have to go out for ziyaarat (visits to significant places), it is best that this is done between Fajar and Zuhr salaah. They should then perform Fajar in Masjidun Nabawi and having visited those places after Fajar, return to perform Zuhr Salaah also in the Masjid.

Hadith No. 8 – Shifa (cure) in the sand of Madinah Munawwarah

Hadhrat Aa'ishah رَضِىَ اللهُ عَنْهَا reports that Rasulullah ﷺ once made dua for the sick,

$$\text{بِسْمِ اللهِ تُرَابُ أَرْضِنَا بِرِيْقِ بَعْضِنَا شِفَاءً لِمَرِيْضِنَا بِاِذْنِ رَبِّنَا}$$

'In the name of Allah, the dust from our earth mixed with our saliva is a healing for our sick with the permission of our Rabb.'"

Whenever someone became ill or injured, Rasulullah ﷺ used to do as is related in this Hadith. Rasulullah ﷺ used to wet his finger with his mubaarak saliva, then rub it in the sand of Madinah and apply it to the injured portion of the body while reading this dua.

    Nabi ﷺ once visited the people of the Banu Haarith where the people were sick. Rasulullah ﷺ asked, "How are you?" They replied: "We suffer from fever." Rasulullah ﷺ then said: "You live near Sa'eeb. Take the dust from its soil and place it in water. Then apply your saliva to it while you read:

$$\text{بِسْمِ اللهِ تُرَابُ أَرْضِنَا بِرِيْقِ بَعْضِنَا شِفَاءً لِمَرِيْضِنَا بِاِذْنِ رَبِّنَا}$$

'In the name of Allah, the dust from our earth mixed with our saliva is a healing for our sick with the permission of our Rabb.'

The people of Banu Haaris did as advised and were healed.

In another Hadith, Saabit bin Qays رضي الله عنه reports that Rasulullah ﷺ said: "The sand of Madinah Munawwarah heals leprosy." As for my humble self[1], I have found that the sand of Madinah Munawwarah even has healing powers against plague. In Wafaaul-Wafaa another Hadith is reported where Rasulullah ﷺ said: "I swear by Him in whose hand lies my life, that the sand of Madinah Munawwarah is a healing medicine for every illness."

Hadith No. 9 – Passing away in Madinah Shareef

Hadhrat Ibn Umar رضي الله عنه reports that Rasulullah ﷺ said: "Whoever has the means to die in Madinah Shareef, let him die there for I shall intercede on behalf of everyone who dies there." [Tirmizi]

Many Sahaabah *(radiyallahu anhum)* have quoted this Hadith that Nabi ﷺ said, "Whosoever is able to die in Madinah Munawwarah, should die in Madinah, for I am a witness for all those who die in Madinah." (Targheeb)

My respected elder, Sayyid Ahmad Madani *(rahmatullahi alayh)*, the founder of Madrasah Uloomush Shar'iyya in Madinah Munawwarah, and the elder brother of Shaikhul Arabi Wal Ajam, Hadhrat Moulana Husain Ahmad Madani *(rahmatullahi alayh)* always said, "It is my heart-felt desire to travel to India just once to meet my beloved friends but I am now old and I fear that I may die outside Madinah."

My honoured ustaaz, Hadhrat Moulana Khalil Ahmad Sahaaranpuri *(rahmatullahi alayh)* always used to make dua at the Multazam that, "O Allah, grant me death in Madinah Shareef."

---

[1] *Hadhrat Shaikh Muhammad Zakariyya Kandhlawi (rahmatullahi alayh)*

The dua of Hadhrat Umar رضي الله عنه is well known,

اَللّٰهُمَّ ارْزُقْنِيْ شَهَادَةً فِيْ سَبِيْلِكَ وَاجْعَلْ مَوْتِيْ بِبَلَدِ رَسُوْلِكَ

"O Allah, grant me martyrdom in Your path and let me die in the town of Your Rasul ﷺ."

Outwardly, Hadhrat Umar رضي الله عنه seemed to have made dua for two things which would have been difficult to attain together, because he lived in Madinah Munawwarah which was Darul Islam, thus being far from the idolaters and enemies of Islam, away from the battlefields, in a place where even shaytaan could not rule. Here to die the death of a martyr seemed very remote. However, when Allah Ta'ala desires something to take place, He prepares the means. Thus, whilst he was among the Sahaabah (*radiyallahu anhum*) in the Masjid of Madinah Munawwarah, during the salaah, he attained martyrdom at the hands of a fire worshipper called Abu Lu'lu.

Yahya bin Sa'eed رضي الله عنه relates: "Once in the presence of Rasulullah ﷺ, a grave was being dug for someone. A man came along and said: 'What an unseemly place for a Muslim to be buried!' Rasulullah ﷺ said: 'What an unsuitable thing for you to say!'"

Rasulullah ﷺ probably meant that the grave of a Muslim should not be called a bad place, because it is actually a garden of paradise. The man replied, 'My intention was that this man died at home, whereas it would have been so much more virtuous had he become a martyr who died in the path of Allah.' Rasulullah ﷺ replied: 'Indeed there is no death more full of virtue than the death of a martyr, yet there is no place more beloved on the face of the earth I prefer for my grave to be than the earth of Madinah.' Rasulullah ﷺ repeated these words three times." (Mishkaat)

What greater fortune can there be for any Muslim than to die with Imaan in Madinah Munawwarah, lying in Jannatul Baqee where the family and companions of Rasulullah ﷺ lie and where, except for two, all his respected wives are buried!

Imaam Maalik *(rahmatullahi alayh)* reports that ten thousand Sahaabah are buried there. How fortunate indeed is he who is buried there where countless mercies descend continuously!

Ibn Najjaar *(rahmatullahi alayh)* reports that Rasulullah ﷺ said: "There are two graveyards on earth shining in the eyes of those in the heavens, as the moon and sun shine for those on the earth. They are the graveyard of Baqee and the graveyard of Asqalaan[1]."

Ka'b Ahbaar, who was a great scholar of the Torah says that it is written therein that Baqee is like a dome upon which special angels are placed and when it is filled it turns over into paradise.

Rasulullah ﷺ said: "On the day of Qiyaamah my grave shall be opened first and I shall step forth, then Abu Bakr ؓ and then Umar ؓ. Then I shall proceed to Baqee and take all its inmates with me. Then we shall await the inmates of the graveyard of Makkah, who will meet me halfway between Makkah and Madinah."

---

[1] *Asqalaan is a coastal city in Palestine near the Gaza Strip. Rasulullah ﷺ made du'a and said thrice, "May Allah Ta'ala have mercy on the people of the graveyard." When asked about which graveyard he was referring to, Rasulullah ﷺ mentioned, "The graveyard in Asqalaan." (Sunan Sa'eed bin Mansoor # 2415). Hadhrat Umar ؓ narrates that once I heard Rasulullah ﷺ speaking about the inmates of a certain graveyard and making lots of dua for them. When asked about it Rasulullah ﷺ mentioned that they were the martyrs of the graveyard of Asqalaan. They will go to Jannah like a bride goes to her groom. (M. Abu Ya'laa # 175)*

In the City of Rasulullah

اِلٰهِيْ نَجِّنِيْ مِنْ كُلِّ ضِيْقٍ فَاَنْتَ اِلٰهُنَا مَوْلَى الْجَمِيْعِ

O Allah! Save me from every difficulty for You are our Rabb and the Rabb of everyone.

وَ هَبْ لِيْ فِيْ الْمَدِيْنَةِ مُسْتَقِرًّا وَرِزْقًا ثُمَّ دَفْنًا فِي الْبَقِيْعِ

Grant me a place to stay and sustenenace in Madinah and burial in Jannatul Baqee

CHAPTER Six

Virtues of Durood & Salaam

Allah Ta'ala has prescribed different azkaar for different occasions. The most virtuous zikr for the visitor to Madinah Munawwarah is the recitation of Durood Shareef. All our pious elders have stressed this point in particular. The more Durood one recites in Madinah Shareef the better.

Usually, the tilaawat of the Qur-aan Shareef is more rewarding than other types of zikr except at certain occassions e.g. on a Friday night, Durood Shareef is more rewarding than tilaawat of the Qur-aan Shareef. Similarly, whilst travelling to Madinah Munawwarah, reciting Durood Shareef is more rewarding than even tilaawat of the Qur-aan-e-Majeed.[1]

---

[1] *Fazaail-e-Haj*

In the City of Rasulullah ﷺ

Whilst walking, waiting, sitting, standing, travelling, etc. we should keep our tongues busy in the recitation of Durood Shareef with full focus. This will bring about great rewards for us as well as earn the happiness of Rasulullah ﷺ.

Allah Ta'ala says in the Qur-aan Shareef:

إِنَّ اللّٰهَ وَمَلٰٓئِكَتَهٗ يُصَلُّوْنَ عَلَى النَّبِيِّ يٰٓاَيُّهَا الَّذِيْنَ اٰمَنُوْا صَلُّوْا عَلَيْهِ وَسَلِّمُوْا تَسْلِيْمًا

Verily, Allah Ta'ala and His angels send durood on Rasulullah ﷺ. O you who believe! Send durood on him, and greet him with a good salutation.

What virtue could be greater than the fact that Allah Ta'ala and His angels join the believers in sending durood and salaams upon Nabi Muhammad ﷺ?

خدا کے طالب دیدار حضرت موسیٰ   تمہارا لیجے، خدا آپ طالب دیدار

Moosa (alayhis salaam) was indeed desirous of seeing Allah Ta'ala, and as for you, Allah Himself was desirous of meeting you

The rewards for reciting durood shareef upon Rasulullah ﷺ are numerous. Many Ahaadith of Rasulullah ﷺ explain the great virtues of reciting durood shareef. Below are some virtues mentioned by Hadhrat Shaikhul Hadeeth, Moulana Muhammad Zakariyya, (rahmatullahi alayh) in his book 'Fazaail-e-Durood'.

One Durood earns ten blessings

Hadhrat Abu Hurayrah رَضِىَ اللهُ عَنْهُ says that Rasulullah ﷺ said, "Whoever sends one durood upon me, Allah Ta'ala showers ten blessings upon him."

One blessing and mercy from Allah Ta'ala is sufficient for the whole world, let alone ten blessings in return for sending durood once. What greater virtue could there be for durood? How fortunate are those pious people who send 125 000 Duroods upon Rasulullah ﷺ every day.

Rasulullah ﷺ said, "Whoever sends durood upon me once, Allah Ta'ala sends ten mercies upon him. It is now your choice to send little or as much as you wish."

One Durood earns ten blessings and removes ten sins

Hadhrat Anas رَضِىَ اللهُ عَنْهُ narrates that Rasulullah ﷺ said, "The person in whose presence I am mentioned should send durood upon me. Whoever sends durood upon me once, Allah Ta'ala sends ten blessings upon him." In one Hadith, Rasulullah ﷺ said, "Whoever sends one durood upon me, Allah Ta'ala sends ten blessings upon him, forgives ten of his sins and raises his status (position) ten times."

Rasulullah ﷺ said, "Whoever sends 10 durood upon me, Allah Ta'ala will shower 100 blessings upon him. Whoever sends 100 durood upon me, Allah Ta'ala will send 1000 blessings upon him, and whoever sends more due to his love and devotion, I shall intercede for him on the Day of Qiyaamah and I will be a witness for him."

A Sahaabi ﷺ says, "From amongst four or five of us, at least one of us would always remain with Rasulullah ﷺ to attend to his needs. One day Rasulullah ﷺ went into a garden and I followed him. Rasulullah ﷺ performed salaah there and made sajdah for such a long time that I feared Rasulullah ﷺ had passed away. I began crying due to this fear and went close to Rasulullah ﷺ. As Rasulullah ﷺ got up from sajdah, he asked, 'O Abdur Rahmaan, what is the matter?' I replied, 'O Messenger of Allah, you performed such a long sajdah that I feared you had passed away.' Rasulullah ﷺ replied, 'Allah Ta'ala has given me a favour with regards to my followers. Showing thanks for this favour, I made this sajdah. Allah Ta'ala has informed me that whoever sends one durood upon me, He will record ten good deeds for him and forgive ten of his sins."

Those who send Durood are closest to Nabi ﷺ

Hadhrat Abdullah ibn Mas'ood ﷺ narrates that Rasulullah ﷺ said, "Indeed, those closest to me on the Day of Qiyaamah will be those who sent durood upon me the most." In a Hadith of Hadhrat Anas ﷺ, it is narrated that at every stage on the Day of Qiyaamah, the closest person to Rasulullah ﷺ shall be that person who sends the most durood upon him. It has also been narrated that Rasulullah ﷺ said, "Send durood upon me abundantly, for you shall first be questioned regarding me in the grave." In another Hadith, it is narrated, "Sending durood upon me shall be a source of light for the darkness of the Bridge on the Day of Qiyaamah. Whoever wishes his deeds to be weighed in a very large scale should send durood upon me abundantly."

Hadhrat Umar رَضِىَاللّٰهُعَنْهُ narrates that Rasulullah ﷺ said, "Beautify your gatherings with durood. Sending durood upon me shall be a light for you on the Day of Qiyaamah."

Allaamah Sakhaawi *(rahmatullahi alayh)* narrates that sending durood in abundance means at least 300 times daily. Moulana Rashid Ahmad Gangohi *(rahmatullahi alayh)* would also instruct his students to send durood at least 300 times daily.

Rasulullah ﷺ said, "Whoever sends durood upon me in a book (i.e. in writing), the angels shall continue sending blessings upon him as long as my name remains in this book."

Rasulullah ﷺ said, "The person who sends 100 durood upon me daily, 100 of his needs shall be fulfilled; thirty of this world and the remaining of the Hereafter."

An angel conveys our Durood to Nabi ﷺ

Hadhrat Ammaar ibn Yaasir رَضِىَاللّٰهُعَنْهُ narrates that Rasulullah ﷺ said, "Verily, Allah Ta'ala has appointed an angel at my grave. He has given him the ability to hear the speech of the whole creation. Until the Day of Qiyaamah there will no person who sends durood upon me except that this angel delivers to me the durood of this person with his name and his father's name, saying, 'The son of so-and-so person has sent durood upon you." Rasulullah ﷺ then said, "In reward for every blessing, Allah Ta'ala sends ten mercies upon him."

Another Hadith mentions that Allah Ta'ala has granted one of the angels the power to hear the speech of the whole creation. This angel will remain at Rasulullah's ﷺ grave until the Day of Qiyaamah. Whenever someone sends durood upon Rasulullah ﷺ, this angel mentions that person by name with his father's name informing Rasulullah ﷺ that this person has sent durood upon him. Allah Ta'ala has promised Rasulullah ﷺ that He shall send ten blessings upon the person who sends one durood upon him.

Rasulullah ﷺ is reported to have said, "Whoever sends durood upon me during the day or night of Friday, Allah Ta'ala will fulfil 100 of his needs. He appoints an angel to convey it to me in my grave, just as you present gifts to one another."

Rasulullah ﷺ hears the Durood at his Grave

Hadhrat Abu Hurayrah ؓ narrates that Rasulullah ﷺ said, "Whoever sends durood upon me by my grave, I hear his durood and whenever durood is sent upon me from a distance, it is brought to me."

Time for sending Durood

Hadhrat Ubayy ibn Ka'b ؓ says, "I asked, 'O Rasulullah ﷺ, I wish to send durood upon you in abundance. How much of the time, which I set aside for dua, should I engage in durood?' Rasulullah ﷺ replied, 'As much as you desire.' I asked, 'One quarter?' Rasulullah ﷺ replied, 'As much as you desire, and if you read more than that, it shall be better for you.' I then asked, 'A half?' Rasulullah ﷺ again said, 'As much as you desire. If you read more than that, it shall be better for you.' I asked, 'Two thirds?' Rasulullah ﷺ replied, 'As much as you desire. If you read more than that, it shall be better for you.' I said, 'I shall spend all my time sending durood upon you.' Rasulullah ﷺ said, 'In that case, all your worries will be removed and your sins will be forgiven.'"

Hadhrat Ubayy رضي الله عنه had set aside some time for dua. He wished to send durood in abundance. He asked how much of this time should he use for sending durood (for example, out of two hours set aside for dua, how much time should be used for sending durood and salaam?) A person asked, "O Messenger of Allah! How would it be if I were to spend all my time in sending durood upon you?" Rasulullah ﷺ replied, "In that case, Allah Ta'ala shall suffice for all your needs in this life and the Hereafter."

Intercession of Nabi ﷺ through Durood

Hadhrat Abu Darda رضي الله عنه narrates that Nabi ﷺ said, "Whoever sends durood upon me ten times in the morning and ten times in the evening, I will intercede on his behalf on the Day of Qiyaamah." Hadhrat Abu Bakr رضي الله عنه narrates that Rasulullah ﷺ said, "Whoever sends durood upon me, I shall intercede for him on the Day of Qiyaamah."

Nabi ﷺ begs forgiveness for the reciter of Durood

Hadhrat Aa'ishah رضي الله عنها narrates that Rasulullah ﷺ said, "No servant sends durood upon me except that an angel goes up with these durood, presenting them before Allah Ta'ala. Our Rabb most High then orders, 'Take these duroods to the grave of my servant, who shall ask for forgiveness on behalf of the sender and who shall be pleased with this.'"

On the Day of Qiyaamah, a certain believer will have few good deeds. Rasulullah ﷺ will place a small piece of paper the size of a fingertip on the scale, causing the scale of good deeds to become heavy. The believer will say, "May my parents be sacrificed for your sake. Who are you? How beautiful is your appearance and character?" Rasulullah ﷺ will reply, "I am your Nabi and these are the durood that you sent to me. I have paid you in your time of need."

Rewards for sending Durood

Some of the rewards for sending durood on Rasulullah ﷺ are as follows;

1. Allah Ta-ala sends blessings upon the reader
2. The Malaaikah send blessings upon him
3. Rasulullah ﷺ himself sends blessings
4. The reciter's sins are forgiven
5. His deeds are cleansed
6. His status is increased
7. The reader's good deeds will weighed heavily in the scale
8. He will be saved from difficulty
9. Rasulullah ﷺ will be a witness for him on the Day of Qiyaamah
10. He will receive the intercession of Rasulullah ﷺ
11. He will attain Allah Ta'ala's pleasure
12. Allah Ta'ala's mercy will descend upon the reader
13. He will be saved from the anger of Allah Ta'ala

14. He will enjoy the shade of Allah Ta'ala's Throne on the Day of Qiyaamah
15. He will be blessed with the honour of being present at the Pond (Al-Kawsar)
16. He will be protected from the thirst on the Day of Qiyaamah
17. He will be freed from the fire of Jahannam and
18. He will see his abode in Jannah before death.

Sending durood is a charity, a means of attaining purity and one is granted blessings in wealth. It is a means of fulfillment for more than a hundred needs. It is an act of worship and the most beloved of deeds to Allah Ta'ala. It is the beauty of all gatherings. It removes poverty and is a means of all goodness. The sender of durood will be the closest to Rasulullah ﷺ on the Day of Qiyaamah. The reader, his children and grandchildren will derive benefit, and likewise the person to whom the reward of the durood has been gifted (esaal-e-sawaab). It is a means of acquiring closeness to Allah Ta'ala and His Noble Messenger ﷺ. Indeed, it is a light and a means of overpowering your enemy.

Durood upon Rasulullah ﷺ is a great light. It is a business wherein there is no loss. Sending durood and salaams has remained the daily practice of the friends of Allah Ta'ala. Be regular in sending durood and salaams upon him. You will be freed from Jahannam, your deeds will be purified, your hopes will be fulfilled, your heart will be brightened, you will earn the pleasure of Allah Ta'ala and you will be at ease on the terrible Day of Qiyaamah.

يَا رَبِّ صَلِّ وَسَلِّمْ دَائِمًا أَبَدًا عَلَى حَبِيبِكَ خَيْرِ الْخَلْقِ كُلِّهِمْ

Occasions for sending Durood

Imaam Sakhaawi *(rahmatullahi alayh)* gathered all the various forms of Durood Shareef in a special chapter of his book 'Qowlul Badee'. He also mentions the special occasions on which they should be recited. Among those moments are the following; after performing wudhu and tayammum; after a compulsory ghusl; before, during and after salaah.

He further mentions that it is Sunnah to recite Durood Shareef after Fajar and Maghrib Salaah; after recitation of the Tashahhud; in Qunoot; when standing up to perform Tahajjud Salaah; when passing any Masjid; when seeing a Masjid; on entering a Masjid; on leaving a Masjid; after answering the azaan; on Friday; the night preceding Friday; during the khutbah for Jumu'ah; on the two Eids; between the takbeers in the Janaazah Salaah; when the dead is placed in his grave; during the month of Sha'baan; when one first sees the Ka'bah; when climbing Mount Safa and Marwa; during the Haj rituals; on completing the Labbaik; when kissing the Black Stone (Hajrul Aswad); while attaching one's body and chest to the Multazam; on the eve of Arafah; in the Masjid at Mina. The visitor to Madinah Munawwarah should recite Durood Shareef when his eyes first fall on Madinah Munawwarah, when visiting the grave of Rasulullah ﷺ; when leaving Madinah Munawwarah; when passing any of the places which Rasulullah ﷺ used to visit; e.g. Badr, etc.

Durood Shareef should also be recited at the time of slaughtering animals; when making a business transaction; when making a will; when reciting a Nikah Khutbah; during the early and late part of each day; at the time of going to sleep; on setting out on a journey; when mounting or boarding a vehicle; when suffering from insomnia (sleeplessness); on going to the market place; when entering the home; when commencing the writing of a book; when one feels sad, restless or experiences hardship or poverty; when drowning takes place; when there is an epidemic; on commencing and completing a dua; during the course of the dua; when the ear buzzes; when the foot becomes numb; when sneezing; when having misplaced something; when seeing a pleasant thing; when repenting or committing a sin; when in need of anything and on every good occasion.

When one is accused of something unpleasant and he is innocent, Durood Shareef should be recited. When meeting friends; when joining and leaving a gathering; when completing a full recitation of the Qur-aan; when making dua for memorising the Qur-aan; on starting any lecture and whenever the name of Rasulullah ﷺ is mentioned.

Durood Shareef should not be left out when knowledge is being taught, when a Hadith is being recited and when the name of Rasulullah ﷺ is being written.

يَا رَبِّ صَلِّ وَ سَلِّمْ دَائِمًا اَبَدًا عَلٰي حَبِيْبِكَ خَيْرِ الْخَلْقِ كُلِّهِمْ

Different types of Durood with special virtues

There are many different types of Durood mentioned in the books of Hadith. Hadhrat Shaikhul Hadeeth, Moulana Zakariyya Saahib (rahmatullahi alayh) has included a chapter in his book Fazaail-e-Durood where he quotes 40 Ahaadith with different forms of durood from the book Zaadus Saeed written by Hadhrat Moulana Ashraf Ali Thaanwi (rahmatullahi alayh). These 40 duroods have now been published separately and widely spread in the Ummah. One may keep a pocket size copy with him and recite it as often as possible.

One may recite whichever durood one feels comfortable with reciting. If possible, one may keep on changing the forms of durood so that one attains all the special virtues mentioned in the Hadith. Some forms of durood with their virtues are mentioned below:

1. Durood that has the reward of charity

اَللّٰهُمَّ صَلِّ عَلٰی (سَیِّدِنَا وَ مَوْلَانَا) مُحَمَّدٍ عَبْدِكَ وَ رَسُوْلِكَ وَ صَلِّ عَلَی الْمُؤْمِنِیْنَ وَ الْمُؤْمِنَاتِ وَ الْمُسْلِمِیْنَ وَ الْمُسْلِمَاتِ

Hadhrat Abu Sa'eed Khudri ؓ narrates that Rasulullah ﷺ said, "If a Muslim does not have anything to give in charity, he should read this durood which shall be a charity for this person." He also said, "The believer is never satisfied with good actions until he reaches Jannah."

2. Durood-e-Ebrahim

اَللّٰهُمَّ صَلِّ عَلٰی (سَیِّدِنَا وَ مَوْلَانَا) مُحَمَّدٍ وَّ عَلٰی اٰلِ (سَیِّدِنَا وَ مَوْلَانَا) مُحَمَّدٍ كَمَا صَلَّیْتَ عَلٰی (سَیِّدِنَا) إِبْرَاهِیْمَ وَ عَلٰی اٰلِ (سَیِّدِنَا) إِبْرَاهِیْمَ اِنَّكَ حَمِیْدٌ مَّجِیْدٌ اَللّٰهُمَّ بَارِكْ عَلٰی (سَیِّدِنَا وَ مَوْلَانَا) مُحَمَّدٍ وَّ عَلٰی اٰلِ (سَیِّدِنَا وَ مَوْلَانَا) مُحَمَّدٍ كَمَا بَارَكْتَ عَلٰی اٰلِ (سَیِّدِنَا) إِبْرَاهِیْمَ وَ عَلٰی اٰلِ (سَیِّدِنَا) إِبْرَاهِیْمَ اِنَّكَ حَمِیْدٌ مَّجِیْدٌ

This is the most virtous of all duroods

3. **Two short forms of Durood**

$$وَ صَلَّى اللهُ عَلَى النَّبِيِّ الْأُمِّيِّ$$

$$بِسْمِ اللهِ وَ السَّلَامُ عَلَى رَسُوْلِ اللهِ$$

4. **Durood that will tire out 70 angels for a 1000 days**

$$جَزَى اللهُ عَنَّا نَبِيَّنَا (سَيِّدَنَا وَ مَوْلَانَا) مُحَمَّدًا صَلَّى اللهُ عَلَيْهِ وَ سَلَّمَ بِمَا هُوَ اَهْلُهُ$$

One who recites this durood will tire out 70 angels for a 1000 days because of writing down the sawaab for the reciter

5. **Durood to recite 80 times after Asar on a Friday**

Hadhrat Abu Hurayrah ﷺ narrates that Rasulullah ﷺ said, "Whoever recites the following durood 80 times before getting up from his place after the Asar Salaah on a Friday, 80 years of his sins will be forgiven and he will be granted the reward of 80 years of Ibaadat (worship):

$$اَللّٰهُمَّ صَلِّ عَلَى مُحَمَّدٍ النَّبِيِّ الْأُمِّيِّ وَعَلَى اٰلِهٖ وَسَلِّمْ تَسْلِيْمًا$$

O Allah, send durood and salaam on Muhammad ﷺ, the unlettered Prophet ﷺ, and upon his family and send the best salaam.

6. Durood of Imaam Shafee *(rahmatullahi alayh)*

Someone saw Imaam Shafee *(rahmatullahi alayh)* in a dream after he passed away and he mentioned to this person, "Allah Ta'ala forgave me and ordered that I be taken to Jannah with great honour and dignity. This was the reward for reciting this durood."

اَللّٰهُمَّ صَلِّ عَلٰى (سَيِّدِنَا وَ مَوْلَانَا) مُحَمَّدٍ كُلَّمَا ذَكَرَهُ الذَّاكِرُوْنَ وَ صَلِّ عَلٰى مُحَمَّدٍ كُلَّمَا غَفَلَ عَنْ ذِكْرِهِ الْغَافِلُوْنَ

Durood which will be measured to its fullest amount

Hadhrat Abu Hurayrah (radhiyallahu anhu) reports that Rasulullah (sallallahu alayhi wasallam) said, "Whoever desires that his deeds be measured in the fullest (on the scale of good deeds) when he sends durood on my household should read this durood."

اَللّٰهُمَّ صَلِّ عَلٰى مُحَمَّدٍ النَّبِيِّ الْأُمِّيِّ وَ اَزْوَاجِهِ اُمَّهَاتِ الْمُؤْمِنِيْنَ وَ ذُرِّيَّتِهِ وَ اَهْلِ بَيْتِهِ كَمَا صَلَّيْتَ عَلٰى إِبْرَاهِيْمَ وَ عَلٰى اٰلِ إِبْرَاهِيْمَ اِنَّكَ حَمِيْدٌ مَجِيْدٌ

Hadhrat Ali (radhiyallahu anhu) has narrated that Rasulullah (sallallahu alayhi wasallam) said, "Whoever sends 100 durood upon me on a Friday will be granted such light on the Day of Qiyaamah that would suffice for the entire creation."

CHAPTER Seven

Jannatul Baqee
(The Graveyard of Madinah)

On Friday morning after conveying our salaams at the Raudha Mubaarak and performing Ishraaq Salaah in Masjidun Nabawi, we proceeded towards Jannatul Baqee, the graveyard of Madinah Munawwarah. Indeed after the graves of the Ambiyaa *(alayhimus salaam)* this is the most virtuous of all graveyards. The earth in this area is filled with treasures of Imaan, Islam, ikhlaas and truth. What a treasure lies beneath this ground? How true is the poem of Hadhrat Khawja Azeezul Hasan Majzoob *(rahmatullahi alyah)*;

ز میں آساں کو کھائی کیسی کیسی دفن ہوگانہ کہیں ایسا خزانہ ہر گز

How is it that the earth has consumed the skies, never before was there such a treasure buried beneath the earth

If one is well versed with the mubaarak life of Rasulullah ﷺ and his illustrious Sahaabah *(radiyallahu anhum)*, one will shiver on every step he takes in Jannatul Baqee. Your tears will saturate the ground beneath you. Every space in this graveyard shouts out the calls of Imaan, A'amaal, Jihaad and Muhabbat (love). Beneath every mound of sand around you lies the most valuable treasure of Islam.

Hadhrat Shaikhul Hadith, Moulana Muhammad Zakariyya *(rahmatullahi alayh)* would advise the visitor to Madinah Munawwarah as follows:

"Visit Jannatul Baqee daily. The people of Madinah Munawwarah should do so every Friday. To do so daily is mustahab and especially on Fridays, but before going to Jannatul Baqee, first make salaam at the grave of Rasulullah ﷺ. Many Sahaabah *(radiyallahu anhum)* are buried in Jannatul Baqee. Some Historians say that there are about 10 000 Sahaabah *(radiyallahu anhum)* buried here. Make dua for all of the inmates of Baqee. It is mustahab to greet Rasulullah ﷺ everyday as well as those buried in Baqee. Hadhrat Aa'ishah ﷺ says, 'Whenever Rasulullah ﷺ used to come to my house, he would always visit Jannatul Baqee first.'"

Entering Jannatul Baqee

We slowly entered Jannatul Baqee reciting the masnoon dua;

اَلسَّلَامُ عَلَيْكُمْ اَهْلَ الدِّيَارِ مِنَ الْمُؤْمِنِيْنَ وَالْمُسْلِمِيْنَ وَ اِنَّا اِنْ شَآءَ اللهُ بِكُمْ لَاحِقُوْنَ نَسْأَلُ اللهَ لَنَا وَ لَكُمُ الْعَافِيَةَ

Peace be upon you, O people of this dwelling, from those who have brought Imaan and Islam. Insha Allah we will be joining you soon. We ask Allah Ta'ala for aafiyat (ease) for you and for us.

This is the place which every Muslim yearns for from the bottom of his heart. If only death would come to us in Madinah Munawwarah and our burial could take place in this garden of Jannah.

وَ هَبْ لِيْ فِى الْمَدِيْنَةِ مُسْتَقِرًّا   وَرِزْقًا ثُمَّ دَفْنًا فِى الْبَقِيْعِ

Grant me a place to stay with sustenenace in Madinah and burial in Jannatul Baqee

Ahl-e-Bayt (the family of Rasulullah ﷺ)

We first visited the graves of the Ahl-e-Bayt (the family of Rasulullah ﷺ) on the right hand side of the graveyard near the entrance. Here the uncle of Rasulullah ﷺ, Hadhrat Abbaas ibnu Abdil Muttalib رضى الله عنه is buried. The leader of the women of Jannah, Hadhrat Faatimah رضى الله عنها is also buried here, about whom Nabi ﷺ mentioned, "Faatimah is from me and I am from her." Next to Hadhrat Faatimah رضى الله عنها is her son Hadhrat Hasan ibn Ali رضى الله عنه and then is her grandson Ali ibnul Husain, Zainul Abideen (*rahmatullahi alayh*. Next to him is Muhammad Al-Baaqir (*rahmatullahi alayh*) and Ja'far As-Saadiq (*rahmatullahi alayh*). This is the area where the beloved family of Rasulullah ﷺ lay buried.

After making salaam and reciting Surah Ikhlaas eleven times, we moved forward to the graves of the remainder of the Banaat-e-Taahiraat (The pure daughters of Rasulullah ﷺ).

The Daughters of Rasulullah ﷺ

In the first enclosure at the entrance of Jannatul Baqee lie buried the remainder of the Banaat-e-Taahiraat (the daughters of Rasulullah ﷺ) viz;
1. Hadhrat Ruqayyah رضي الله عنها
2. Hadhrat Umm-e-Kulsoom رضي الله عنها
3. Hadhrat Zaynab رضي الله عنها.

Hadhrat Ruqayyah رضي الله عنها and Hadhrat Umme Kulsoom رضي الله عنها were both married to Hadhrat Usmaan رضي الله عنه one after the other. Hadhrat Ruqayyah رضي الله عنها passed away in the year 2 A.H. when the Sahaabah (radiyallahu anhum) were returning from the Battle of Badr. Thereafter Hadhrat Umme Kulsoom رضي الله عنها married Hadhrat Usmaan رضي الله عنه. She passed away in the year 9 A.H. Hadhrat Zaynab رضي الله عنها was the eldest daughter of Rasulullah ﷺ. She was married to her cousin, Abul Aas bin Rabi رضي الله عنه. She passed away in the year 8 A.H.

Azwaaj-e-Mutahharaat – The pure wives of Rasulullah ﷺ

As you move a little forward, there is another enclosure that marks the graves of the Azwaaj-e-Mutahharaat. With the exception of Hadhrat Khadijah رضي الله عنها[1] and Hadhrat Maymoonah رضي الله عنها,[2] all the other Ummahaatul Mu'mineen (the mothers of the believers) are buried at this

---

[1] *Hadhrat Khadijah رضي الله عنها is buried in Jannatul Mu'alla in Makkah Mukarramah*
[2] *Hadhrat Maymoonah رضي الله عنها is buried in a placed called Sarif outside Makkah Mukarramah. Her nikah with Hadhrat Nabi ﷺ also took place at Sarif.*

spot. Those were the pure and chaste women whom Allah Ta'ala had chosen to take care of Rasulullah ﷺ. May Allah Ta'ala reward them with the greatest of rewards. They helped and supported Rasulullah ﷺ in all his matters. Many a times there was no food in their homes. They suffered poverty and hunger. Hadhrat Aaishah رضي الله عنها says, "At times we had seen the third month without having any cooked meals in our homes. We sufficed on dates and water for survival." They sacrificed all their comforts and supported Nabi ﷺ in his mission of spreading Islam. May Allah Ta'ala be pleased with them all.

The names of the Azwaaj-e-Mutahaarat buried here are as follows:

1. Hadhrat Aaishah رضي الله عنها
2. Hadhrat Hafsah رضي الله عنها
3. Hadhrat Safiyyah رضي الله عنها
4. Hadhrat Saudah رضي الله عنها
5. Hadhrat Umm-e-Salimah رضي الله عنها
6. Hadhrat Umm-e-Habibah رضي الله عنها
7. Hadhrat Zaynab bint Jahsh رضي الله عنها
8. Hadhrat Zaynab bint-e-Khuzaymah رضي الله عنها
9. Hadhrat Juwayriyyah رضي الله عنها

Aqeel ibn Abi Taalib رضي الله عنه, Abu Sufyaan ibnul Haaris رضي الله عنه, Abdullah bin Ja'far رضي الله عنه

At the next enclosure are the graves of three Sahaabah.
1. Aqeel ibn Abi Taalib رضي الله عنه, (the brother of Hadhrat Ali رضي الله عنه)
2. Abu Sufyaan ibnul Haaris رضي الله عنه (the cousin of Rasulullah ﷺ) and

3. Abdullah bin Ja'far ﺭﺿﻲ ﺍﻟﻠﻪ ﻋﻨﻪ. He is the son of Hadhrat Ja'far ﺭﺿﻲ ﺍﻟﻠﻪ ﻋﻨﻪ who was martyred in the Battle of Muta.

Abu Sufyaan Ibnul Haaris ﺭﺿﻲ ﺍﻟﻠﻪ ﻋﻨﻪ is that Sahaabi who in the battle of Hunayn, when everyone deserted Rasulullah ﺻﻠﻰ ﺍﻟﻠﻪ ﻋﻠﻴﻪ ﻭﺳﻠﻢ, never left his side even though his life was at stake. It was indeed a very trying time for the Muslims. One person casually remarked:

"Today we will not be defeated because of small numbers."

This remark, tainted with pride and ostentation, was disliked by Allah Ta'ala. Victory and help is from Allah Ta'ala alone. However, Allah Ta'ala did not like this statement and instead of victory, they first had to see the face of defeat. When the Muslim army reached the valley of Hunayn, the Hawaazin and Saqeef tribes were lying in ambush. Maalik ibn 'Auf had, at the beginning, ordered them to break the sheaths of their swords saying to them that when the Muslim army approaches, the entire army of 20 000 should attack the Muslims all at once. When the Muslim army started to cross that area in the darkness of dawn, 20 000 swords suddenly attacked them. This completely scattered the Muslim army. Only 10-12 loyal and devoted companions remained next to Rasulullah ﺻﻠﻰ ﺍﻟﻠﻪ ﻋﻠﻴﻪ ﻭﺳﻠﻢ. Hadhrat Abu Bakr, 'Umar, Ali, 'Abbaas, Fadl ibn 'Abbaas, Usaamah ibn Zaid ﺭﺿﻲ ﺍﻟﻠﻪ ﻋﻨﻬﻢ and a few others remained at his side. 'Abbaas ﺭﺿﻲ ﺍﻟﻠﻪ ﻋﻨﻪ was holding on to the reins of Rasulullah's ﺻﻠﻰ ﺍﻟﻠﻪ ﻋﻠﻴﻪ ﻭﺳﻠﻢ donkey while Abu Sufyaan ibnul Haaris ﺭﺿﻲ ﺍﻟﻠﻪ ﻋﻨﻪ was holding on to the stirrup.

Next to Hadhrat Abu Sufyaan ibnul Haaris ﺭﺿﻲ ﺍﻟﻠﻪ ﻋﻨﻪ is the grave of Abdullah bin Ja'far ﺭﺿﻲ ﺍﻟﻠﻪ ﻋﻨﻪ the cousin of Hadhrat Hasan and Husain ﺭﺿﻲ ﺍﻟﻠﻪ ﻋﻨﻪ. His father was one of the leaders in the Battle of Muta who lost both his hands in the battle holding up the flag of Islam. In Fazaail-e-

Sadaqaat, Hadhrat Shaikh Zakariyya *(rahmatullahi alayh)* has mentioned some incidents about his sublime generosity.

Imaam Maalik and Imaam Nafi' *(rahmatullahi alayhima)*

A little further away from the grave of Hadhrat Abdullah bin Ja'far رَضِىَ اللّٰهُ عَنْهُ you will find another enclosed area where Imaamu Daril Hijrah, Imaam Maalik ibn Anas *(rahmatullahi alayh)* is buried alongside his ustaaz, Imaam Nafi *(rahmatullahi alayh)*.

Imaam Maalik *(rahmatullahi alayh)* was born in the year 93 A.H. in Madinah Munawwarah, in a pious family who were well-known for their knowledge. He memorised the Qur'aan Shareef in his early childhood and then began to study and memorise Ahaadith. At the tender age of seventeen, he began teaching Hadith. He compiled a book on Hadith called "Mu'atta" which was one of the first books of Hadith pertaining to Fiqh (jurisprudence). It took him eleven years to compile this book. Amongst his illustrious students are Imaam Shaafi *(rahmatullahi alayh)*, Imaam Muhammad *(rahmatullahi alayh)* and Abdullah bin Mubaarak *(rahmatullahi alayh)*.

Imaam Maalik *(rahmatullahi alayh)* was famous for his piety and his strong adherence to the Sunnah. On one occasion he was conducting lessons on Hadith when his face changed colour. On enquiry, the students were told that he was bitten by a scorpion thirteen times but due to respect for the Hadith of Rasulullah ﷺ he did not stop the lesson. He never rode an animal in Madinah Munawwarah saying: "I feel ashamed to ride an animal on the soil where Rasulullah ﷺ placed his mubaarak feet." He passed away at the age of eighty-six in Rabiul Awwal 179 A.H. in Madinah Munawwarah and was buried at the feet of his ustaaz, Imaam Nafi *(rahmatullahi alayh)*.

Imaam Nafi *(rahmatullahi alayh)* is a famous Qaari who is one of the narrators of the seven dialects of Qiraat. He passed away about ten years before Imaam Maalik *(rahmatullahi alayh)*.

He was the leader of the Qurra in Madinah Munawwarah. He resided with the people of Madinah for about seventy years.

Lays ibn Sa'd *(rahmatullahi alayh)* says, "I went for Haj in the year 113 A.H. and the Imaam of Madinah Munawwarah was Imaam Nafi."

Abu Amr *(rahmatullahi alayh)* narrates, "A man who learnt to recite from Imaam Nafi *(rahmatullahi alayh)* said, "When the Imaam spoke, fragrance of musk would emanate from his mouth. I said to him, 'Do you use perfume whenever you sit to recite to the people?' He replied, 'I do not touch perfume, but I saw in a dream that Rasulullah ﷺ, was reciting into my mouth and from that moment I have smelt this fragrance from my mouth.'"

It was once said to Imaam Nafi *(rahmatullahi alayh)*, "How brilliant your face is and how handsome is your physique!" He replied, "How could it not be when Rasulullah ﷺ breathed on me when I recited the Qur-aan (i.e. in the dream)."

The old graveyard of Madinah Munawwarah

As you take a few steps forward, you will come across a piece of land which, according to many Historians, is the area that was originally known as the graveyard of Madinah Munawwarah. Hadhrat Usmaan ibn Mazoon ؓ is buried here. He is that Sahaabi whom Rasulullah ﷺ kissed on his forehead. Next to him is the beloved son of Rasulullah ﷺ, Hadhrat Ibraaheem ؓ for whom Nabi ﷺ teared when he passed away and said, "Our eyes will tear, our hearts will grieve but we will never say anything except what will please

Allah Ta'ala. Indeed we are grieved at your separation O Ibraheem." Next to him is the Faqeeh of this Ummah, Hadhrat Abdullah ibn Masood رضي الله عنه and the conqueror of Iraq, Hadhrat Sa'd bin Abi Waqqaas رضي الله عنه, and many other great Sahaabah of Rasulullah ﷺ.

Abdullah ibn Masood رضي الله عنه is that Sahaabi who was known as the resemblance of Rasulullah ﷺ. The Fiqh of the Hanafi Mazhab is derived mostly from Hadhrat Abdullah ibn Masood رضي الله عنه.

Sa'd bin Abi Waqqaas رضي الله عنه was the uncle of Rasulullah ﷺ. He is that Sahaabi who shot the first arrows in Islam. Nabi ﷺ once said to him, "May my parents be sacrificed for you, O Sa'd." Nabi ﷺ made special dua for him that all his duas should be answered. Hence he became *mustajaabud da'waat*.

Some historians write that Hadhrat As'ad bin Zurarah رضي الله عنه is also buried here. He was the first person from the Ansaar to accept Islam. He had put forward a request to Nabi ﷺ to send someone to Madinah Shareef to teach the Muslims the important teachings of Islam. Hence, Nabi ﷺ sent Hadhrat Abdullah ibn Umme Maktoom رضي الله عنه and Hadhrat Mus'ab bin Umair رضي الله عنه to Madinah Shareef to establish the first maktab or Madrasah. This Madrasah was established in the home of As'ad bin Zurarah رضي الله عنه.

The sun was now shining brightly as we moved forward and the beautiful Green Dome above Masjidun Nabawi could be clearly seen from behind us. Walking inbetween the graves of these great Sahaabah (*radiyallahu anhum ajmaeen*) is indeed a great honour for grave sinners like us. We hope that by standing in the midst of these great personalities, Allah Ta'ala, through His infinite kindness and Mercy will forgive our sins.

Shuhadaa (Martyrs) of Harrah

Along the pathway on the left hand side is a short wall that cordons off the graves of seventy Shuhadaa (martyrs) who were martyred in the Battle of Harrah in the reign of Yazeed in the year 63 A.H. During this battle, the people of Madinah Munawwarah were so frightened that many of them fled. Some remained in their homes, while the horses of Yazid's armies roamed in the Masjid. It was such a battle wherein 1700 Muhaajireen and Ansaar were killed, and more than 10,000 people, apart from women and children, lost their lives.

During that period, Hadhrat Saeed Ibnul Musayyib *(rahmatullahi alayh)* found himself at times completely alone in Masjid-e-Nabawi. He says: "For days on end no one entered the Masjid. During that time I heard the Azaan and the Iqaamah from the grave of Rasulullah ﷺ." [1]

Ameerul Mu'mineen, Hadhrat Usmaan bin Affaan ؓ

Right at the back of Jannatul Baqee lies the grave of the most virtuous of all those buried in Baqee, Hadhrat Usmaan ibn Affaan ؓ. We stood for some time at the grave of this third Khalifah who was assassinated by rebels in his home whilst reciting the Qur-aan Shareef. How fond was Nabi ﷺ of him! On several occasions, Nabi ﷺ praised him for his generous contributions to the Muslims. On the occasion of Hudaybiyyah, when the Muslims received the rumour of his death, Nabi ﷺ took bay'at (pledge of allegiance) from the Sahaabah for

---

[1] *Fazaaile Haj*

jihaad to avenge the death of Hadhrat Usmaan رَضِىَ اللهُ عَنْهُ. At that moment, Nabi صَلَّى اللهُ عَلَيْهِ وَسَلَّمَ said, "Usmaan has gone out for the sake of Allah and His Rasul, therefore, I will take bay'at on his behalf." He then placed his right hand into his left hand and took the pledge on behalf of Hadhrat Usmaan رَضِىَ اللهُ عَنْهُ.

Nabi صَلَّى اللهُ عَلَيْهِ وَسَلَّمَ once said, "My companion in Jannah will be Usmaan." When Hadhrat Umm-e-Kulsoom رَضِىَ اللهُ عَنْهَا, the beloved daughter of Rasulullah صَلَّى اللهُ عَلَيْهِ وَسَلَّمَ passed away, Nabi صَلَّى اللهُ عَلَيْهِ وَسَلَّمَ said, "If I had more daughters, I would have given them all (one by one) in marriage to Usmaan." He was well known by the title Zun Noorain (The possessor of two lights) as he was the only person honoured with the privilege of marrying two daughters of Rasulullah صَلَّى اللهُ عَلَيْهِ وَسَلَّمَ.

Nabi صَلَّى اللهُ عَلَيْهِ وَسَلَّمَ predicted the martyrdom of Hadhrat Usmaan رَضِىَ اللهُ عَنْهُ. Towards the end of his khilaafat, some people objected to certain of his actions. They formed a small group and decided to rebel against him. The Sahaabah *(radiyallahu anhum)* who were governors of the different provinces were consulted regarding what should be done with the rebels. They all felt that the rebels, who were in the minority, should be killed. Hadhrat Usmaan رَضِىَ اللهُ عَنْهُ was very soft and gentle in his approach towards people. He did not want any bloodshed in his khilaafat. He therefore refused all forms of violence.

This approach of Hadhrat Usmaan رَضِىَ اللهُ عَنْهُ made the rebels even bolder. They began to physically harm him by pelting stones at him but he still refused to take revenge or action against these rebels. Several Sahaabah came to fight against them but Hadhrat Usmaan رَضِىَ اللهُ عَنْهُ sent them away, saying, "Whatever Allah Ta'ala has destined will take place."

Eventually the rebels demanded his life. Then too, he addressed them mildly saying, "Why are you demanding my life? I have heard Rasulullah صَلَّى اللهُ عَلَيْهِ وَسَلَّمَ say: 'A person may be killed for one of three reasons: (1) If he has committed adultery, (2) murder or (3) turned away from his Deen.' I have not committed adultery or murder, nor have I turned away from my Deen. Why then are you demanding my life?"

Finally, the rebels surrounded the house of Hadhrat Usmaan رضي الله عنه for forty days and stopped the water supply from reaching his home. When Hadhrat 'Ali رضي الله عنه heard about this, he sent some water to the house of Hadhrat Usmaan رضي الله عنه. However, very little water reached his house as some people were injured whilst trying to take the water to him. Hadhrat Ali رضي الله عنه had ordered his sons, Hasan رضي الله عنه and Husain رضي الله عنه, to guard the house of Hadhrat Usmaan رضي الله عنه. A few other Sahaabah also sent their sons to guard his house. Some of the rebels jumped over the fence from the rear, unnoticed and entered the house of Hadhrat Usmaan رضي الله عنه. He was busy engaged in the recitation of the Qur-aan Shareef when they attacked him. On seeing this, his wife Naailah رضي الله عنها ran forward to protect him. In her effort to save him, the rebels cut off three of her fingers. Hadhrat Usmaan رضي الله عنه was attacked and stabbed to death. He was 82 years old when he was martyred. At the time of his death, he was reciting the Qur-aan Shareef and was also fasting. This happened on a Friday, 18 Zul Hijjah 35 A.H., at the time of Asar. Due to certain circumstances, the Sahaabah *(radiyallahu anhum)* were unable to perform the Janaazah Salaah immediately. It was only on Saturday that a few Sahaabah performed his Janaazah Salaah in secret and buried him without giving him ghusal.[1]

We stood for a long while at the grave of Hadhrat Zun Noorain رضي الله عنه and after making salaam to him walked on further to the grave of Hadhrat Haleemah Sa'diyyah رضي الله عنها, the foster mother of Rasulullah

---

[1] *The law of Islam is that martyrs are buried without ghusal. They will be raised on the day of Qiyaamah with blood flowing from their bodies and this will be a means of great honour for them.*

ﷺ. She was that woman who was honoured to look after Rasulullah ﷺ for four years in his childhood.

Sa'd bin Muaaz رضي الله عنه and Abu Saeed Khudri رضي الله عنه

The last enclosure in Jannatul Baqee marks the graves of two great Sahaabah, viz. Hadhrat Sa'd bin Muaaz رضي الله عنه and Hadhrat Abu Saeed Khudri رضي الله عنه.

Sa'd bin Muaaz رضي الله عنه is that Sahaabi who, on the occasion of Badar, when Nabi ﷺ was looking for the support of the Ansaar, immediately understood what Nabi ﷺ wanted, stood up and delivered the following most inspiring speech.

"O Rasulullah ﷺ! We have affirmed our belief in you, we believe in you, we bear testimony to the fact that whatever you came with is the truth and upon this we had wholeheartedly pledged our absolute submission. O Rasulullah ﷺ! Perhaps you emerged from Madinah Munawwarah with a specific purpose but Allah Ta'ala has brought about something else. So proceed as you deem fit. You may maintain ties with whom you wish and you may sever ties with whomsoever you wish. You may enter into a peace agreement with whom you wish and you may go to war with whom you wish. We are with you all the way. You may take from our wealth whatever you please and you may bestow upon us whatever you please. Whatever you take from our wealth would be dearer to us than what you would leave behind, and whatever you charge us to do we will unquestionably abide by it. If you bid us to set off for Barkul-Ghamaad with you, we will eagerly accompany you. I swear by the Being Who has deputed you with the truth, if you direct us to leap into the ocean we would eagerly hurl ourselves into it and not one of us would be left behind. We do not detest confronting the enemy. Yes, during the heat of battle we are tolerant and we are committed to meet the enemy head-on. We hope Allah Ta'ala will exhibit something of ours that would bring about the coolness of your eyes. So, in the name of Allah, take us along with you."

When Sa'd bin Muaaz رضي الله عنه passed away, the arsh of Allah Ta'ala shook at his demise. In the Battle of Khandaq, he was struck on his jugular by an arrow. He then made the following dua:

> O Allah! If this struggle against the Quraysh is bound to last (for some time) then let me live also accordingly because I have no yearning greater than fighting the people who subjected Your Messenger to such hardship, falsified him and evicted him from the safe Haram. O Allah! If this is the end of the struggle, make this injury a source of my martyrdom and do not take my life away until I am able to cool my eyes with the humiliation of the Banu Qurayzah."

He passed away as a shaheed in the Battle of the Trench.

Hadhrat Abu Sa'eed Al-Khudri رضي الله عنه was a much respected Sahaabi from the Khazraj tribe in Madinah Munawwarah. He was thirteen years old when his father was martyred in the Battle of Uhud at the side of Rasulullah ﷺ. He was present with Nabi ﷺ in the Battle of Khandaq, Treaty of Hudaybiyyah and all the other expeditions thereafter. He narrated 1170 Ahaadith of Rasulullah ﷺ. Most of his time was spent in the Masjid of Rasulullah ﷺ learning Ahaadith. He passed away in Madinah Munawwarah in the year 74 A.H.

When Madinah Munawwarah was under attack in the battle of Harrah, a man came to Hadhrat Abu Saeed Khudhri رضي الله عنه complaining of hardship and difficulty and seeking advice about moving out of Madinah Munawwarah. Hadhrat Abu Sa'eed رضي الله عنه replied: "Never! I shall never give you such advice for I have personally heard Rasulullah ﷺ saying; 'Whoever bears patiently the trials and hardships of Madinah Munawwarah, and suffers patiently the pangs of hunger, for him I shall be an intercessor on the day of Qiyaamah.'"

Men who were true in their promises to Allah Ta'ala

After making salaam and reciting some portions of the Qur-aan Shareef, we turned around and took one glance at the whole graveyard of Baqee. *Allahu Akbar*! How true are the words in which Allah Ta'ala described these men,

$$رِجَالٌ صَدَقُوْا مَا عَاهَدُوا اللّٰهَ عَلَيْهِ$$

Men who were true in their promises to Allah Ta'ala

In Makkah Mukarramah they gave their hands into the mubaarak hand of Rasulullah ﷺ and in Madinah Munawwarah they remain resting at his mubaarak feet. Has the world ever witnessed men of this nature? Men who served Allah's Deen and served Allah's Rasul ﷺ with their wealth, their time and their lives.

As we stood there marvelling at the graves in Baqee, the dua emanated from our hearts, "O Allah, as you have accepted these great men of Islam, grant us also the ability to live and serve Islam and also to die on Islam and Imaan as these Noble men had done." This is the lesson Jannatul Baqee teaches its visitors.

As we walked back silently reciting Surah Yaseen, a sense of deep joy and happiness entered our hearts. For a believer, this is a dream come true. How wonderful it would be if this would be our resting place. If only Allah Ta'ala would accept us to live and die in Madinah

Munawwarah. If only Jannatul Baqee would become our final resting place. Indeed we are not fit to be here. We are not worthy of resting here, but Allah Ta'ala, in His Mercy, blesses people without any credentials and qualifications. We would enjoy the privilege of becoming the neighbours of the Sahaabah ﷺ and the neighbours of Rasulullah ﷺ.

اَللّٰهُمَّ ارْزُقْنِيْ شَهَادَةً فِيْ سَبِيْلِكَ وَاجْعَلْ مَوْتِيْ بِبَلَدِ رَسُوْلِكَ

"O Allah, grant me martyrdom in Your path and let me die in the city of Your Rasul ﷺ."

This was the dua made by Hadhrat 'Umar ﷺ. Allah Ta'ala accepted his dua. May Allah Ta'ala also accept our dua.

In one poem, Qari Siddeeq Ahmad Baandwi (rahmatullahi alayh) mentions the following couplets:

This is my desire, this is my yearning, that my body can also become a patch in the graveyard of Baqee

Hadhrat Shaikh Zakariyya, Hadhrat Moulana Khalil Ahmad Saharanpuri and Hadhrat Moulana Badre Aalam (rahimahumullah)

Above the area where the Azwaaj-e-Mutaharaat are buried, lay the graves of three of our great senior Akaabir of Deoband.

1. Hadhrat Shaikh Zakariyya Kandhlawi *(rahmatullahi alayh)*.
2. Hadhrat Moulana Khalil Ahmad Saharanpuri *(rahmatullahi alayh)*.
3. Hadhrat Moulana Badre Aalam *(rahmatullahi alayh)*.

Hadhrat Moulana Khalil Ahmad Saharanpuri Saahib *(rahmatullahi alayh)* had made special dua at the multazam for death in Madinah Munawwarah. Allah Ta'ala accepted his dua. His favourite student and disciple, Hadhrat Shaikh Zakariyya *(rahmatullahi alayh)* migrated to Madinah Munawwarah towards the end of his life and lived in Madinah and passed away in Madinah Munawwarah.

Hadhrat Moulana Badr-e-Aalam *(rahmatullahi alayh)* migrated to Madinah Shareef many years before that. He would conduct a majlis daily after Asar at his residence. Many South Africans had taken bay'at to him and would regularly write to him. Six months after his demise, they dug his grave to reuse it and found that his body was still intact. After another six months they again dug the grave only to find his body as fresh as the day he had passed away. The authorities then marked this grave that it should not be dug again in the future. Hadhrat Moulana Abraarul Haq Saahib *(rahmatullahi alayh)* investigated this matter and was told by Hadhrat Moulana's family that she feels her husband received this honour because of his exceptional respect he had for the Qur-aan-e-Majeed. He would never stretch his feet towards a Haafiz of the Qur-aan even though the Haafiz was a little child.

Hadhrat Moulana Sa'eed Khan Saahib *(rahmatullahi alayh)* is also one of our senior Ulama who is buried in Jannatul Baqee. Hadhrat Moulana was amongst the senior Akaabir of the work of Da'wat and Tableegh. He was sent to Madinah Munawwarah by Hadhratji Moulana Yusuf Saahib *(rahmatullahi alayh)* to manage the jamaat work in Hejaz. Hadhrat Moulana dedicated his entire life in Madinah Munawwarah and was mainly responsible for the Arabs taking to the work of da'wat.

Towards the end of his life he was forced by the authorities to leave Madinah Shareef but it was the plan of Allah Ta'ala that he will die in Madinah and be buried in Jannatul Baqee. When Allah Ta'ala plans something for someone, who is there to change the plan of Allah Ta'ala. A few days before he passed away he came to Madinah Munawwarah as a visitor and passed away in this beautiful city. He also enjoys the honour of being buried in Jannatul Baqee.

The aunts of Rasulullah ﷺ

On the right hand-side of the graveyard, just before the exit gate, lie the graves of the aunts of Rasulullah ﷺ, Hadhrat Safiyyah رضي الله عنها and Hadhrat Aatiqah رضي الله عنها. We stood a while at these graves and after making salaam and reciting some portions of the Qur-aan Shareef, left the graveyard and moved back towards the Haram Shareef.

Below is a small map of Jannatul Baqee, marking the graves of the Sahaabah *(radiyallahu anhum ajmaeen)*.

Jannatul Baqee

1. Ahl-e-Bayt (family of Rasulullah ﷺ)
2. Daughters of Rasulullah ﷺ
3. Azwaaj-e-Mutaharaat (wives of Rasulullah ﷺ)
4. Aqeel ibn abi Taalib, Abu Sufyaan ibnul Haaris, Abdullah bin Ja'far ؓ
5. Imaam Maalik and Imaam Nafi
6. Ibrahim ؑ (The son of Rasulullah ﷺ) and other senior Sahaabah
7. Martyrs of the Battle of Harrah
8. Hadhrat Usmaan ؓ
9. Haleemah Sa'diyyah ؓ
10. Sa'd bin Muaaz and Abu Saeed Khudri ؓ
11. The aunts of Rasulullah ﷺ

CHAPTER Eight

Masjidul Quba

On Saturday morning, after the Fajar Salaah, we took a taxi from outside the Haram Shareef towards Masjid-e-Quba. This is that place which was blessed with the presence of Rasulullah ﷺ even before the city of Madinah Munawwarah. This is where the first masjid of Islam was built and whose foundation stone was laid by none other than Sayyidul Ambiyaa, Hadhrat Muhammad Mustafa ﷺ.

After the Masjid of Makkah Mukarramah, the Masjid of Madinah Munawwarah and the Masjid in Baitul Muqaddas, the Masjid of Quba is the most important and virtuous. Rasulullah ﷺ has said: "To perform two rakaats of salaah in the Masjid of Quba is more beloved to me than travelling twice to Baitul Muqaddas." [1]

---

[1] *Fathul Baari* #1191

Rasulullah ﷺ liked visiting Quba on Saturdays. He also went there on a Monday and on one occasion went on the 20th of Ramadhaan.

Hadhrat Abdullah bin Umar رضي الله عنه relates: "Rasulullah ﷺ would visit Masjid-e-Quba every Saturday. Sometimes he would go walking and at times he would go mounted on a conveyance. He would then offer two Rakaat Salaah in this Masjid." [1]

Sahal bin Hunaif رضي الله عنه narrates that Rasulullah ﷺ said: "He who performs wudhu at home and performs two Rakaats Salaah in Masjid-e-Quba will acquire the Sawaab of an Umrah." [2]

When going to Masjid-e-Quba, go with deep love and respect and place your forehead on that piece of ground where our beloved Nabi ﷺ and his illustrious Sahaabah had placed their mubaarak foreheads. What a great honour, what a prestige. Breathe deeply in the environment of Quba, this is that area where our Nabi ﷺ also breathed in.

Quba lies approximately three miles south of Madinah Munawwarah. Here, a few families of the Ansaar resided. These inhabitants were predominantly made up of the family of 'Amr bin 'Awf رضي الله عنه and the chieftain of this family was Kulsoom bin Hadam رضي الله عنه. When Rasulullah ﷺ arrived in Quba, he stayed at the house of Kulsoom bin Hadam رضي الله عنه whilst Hadhrat Abu Bakr رضي الله عنه stayed at the house of Khubaib bin Isaaf رضي الله عنه. The Ansaar would come to Rasulullah ﷺ in droves from all around the vicinity and with utmost humility would present themselves to offer their salaams.

---

[1] Saheeh Bukhaari #1193
[2] Ibnu Majah #1412

After the departure of Rasulullah ﷺ from Makkah Mukarramah, Hadhrat Ali رضى الله عنه stayed over in Makkah Mukarramah for three days. After returning the property and wealth of the people entrusted to him by Rasulullah ﷺ, Hadhrat Ali رضى الله عنه also left Makkah Mukarramah, joined Rasulullah ﷺ in Quba and also stayed with Rasulullah ﷺ at the house of Kulsoom bin Hadam رضى الله عنه.

Foundation of Masjid-e-Quba

Subsequent to his arrival in Quba, the first task Rasulullah ﷺ undertook was the laying of the foundation of a Masjid. He brought a stone with his own blessed hands and placed it in the direction of the Qiblah. Hadhrat Abu Bakr رضى الله عنه and then Hadhrat 'Umar رضى الله عنه also placed a stone each in the same direction. After them, the other Sahaabah رضى الله عنهم fetched a stone each and then the actual construction of the Masjid started in earnest. Rasulullah ﷺ would also carry the heavy boulders himself. At times, to clutch it more firmly, he would hold it close to his blessed stomach. The Sahaabah رضى الله عنهم would urge him to leave it but Rasulullah ﷺ would not yield to their appeals.

Men who love cleanliness

The following verses of the Qur-aan were revealed with regards to this masjid:

لَمَسْجِدٌ اُسِّسَ عَلَى التَّقْوٰى مِنْ اَوَّلِ يَوْمٍ اَحَقُّ اَنْ تَقُوْمَ فِيْهِ ۗ فِيْهِ رِجَالٌ يُّحِبُّوْنَ اَنْ يَّتَطَهَّرُوْا ۗ وَاللّٰهُ يُحِبُّ الْمُطَّهِّرِيْنَ

"Surely the Masjid that was erected upon Taqwa (Allah-consciousness) from the first day is more befitting that you stand (for Salaah) within it. In it are men who love (physical and spiritual) cleanliness. And Allah loves those who purify themselves." [Surah Taubah Verse 108]

When this verse was revealed, Rasulullah ﷺ asked 'Amr bin 'Awf رضى الله عنه: "On what type of *tahaarat* (purity) did you attract the praise of Allah?" The people of Bani 'Amr replied: "O Rasulullah ﷺ! After using clods of earth, we make Istinjaa (cleansing of the private parts) with water as well. Perhaps this two fold *tahaarat* (purity) earned the pleasure of Allah Ta'ala, hence, we were praised in the Qur-aan."

Rasulullah ﷺ remarked: "Yes, this is the practice which has attracted Allah's recognition. You should stick firmly to this practice and remain attached to it."

Date of Hijrah

The day Rasulullah ﷺ made his mubaarak presence in Quba during the journey of Hijrah, was a Monday and the date was the 8th Rabiul-Awwal, thirteen years after Prophethood.

According to the scholars of Seerah, Rasulullah ﷺ left Makkah Mukarramah on Thursday 27th Safar. Following his stopover of three days in the cave of Saur, he left for Madinah Munawwarah on Monday, the 1st Rabiul-Awwal. Travelling on the coastal route, Rasulullah ﷺ made his noble appearance in Quba on Monday afternoon the 8th of Rabiul-Awwal.

Following a short stay of a few days in Quba, Rasulullah ﷺ mounted his camel and departed for Madinah Munawwarah on a Friday. En-route lies the locality of Banu Saalim. Since the time of

Jumu'ah had set in, Rasulullah ﷺ performed the Jumu'ah Salaah here. This was the first Khutbah and Jumu'ah in Islam. Today, a masjid by the name Masjid-e-Jumu'ah marks this spot. A very historic *khutbah* (lecture) was delivered on this occasion by Rasulullah ﷺ. The translation of the khutbah is mentioned below;

The topic of this khutbah is "TAQWA"

"All praise is due to Allah. I glorify Him, I beseech His assistance, I beg His forgiveness and I plead for His divine guidance. I believe in Him and I renounce disbelief in Him. In fact I oppose those who disbelieve in Allah. I bear witness that there is none worthy of worship besides Allah, He has no partner and I testify that Muhammad (ﷺ) is His slave and messenger. He was commissioned by Allah Ta'ala (to this earth) with guidance, spiritual radiance and good counsel at a time when the succession of Prophets had terminated and at a time when there was a drought of knowledge and when people were spiritually deviated and close to the day of judgement. He who obeys Allah and His Rasool is rightly guided whilst he who disobeys them has gone astray, transgressed and he is extremely deviated.

I advise you to adhere firmly to Taqwa (Allah-consciousness) because the best advice one Muslim can impart to another Muslim is that he persuades him to harbour concern for the hereafter and that he enjoins him to adhere to Taqwa.

So beware of that which Allah Ta'ala Himself has warned you about. There is no better advice than Taqwa. Certainly the Taqwa of Allah Ta'ala and fear for Him is an ideal benefactor for the hereafter.

He who rectifies his external as well as his internal affairs with Allah Ta'ala and his intention is nothing but the pleasure of Allah Ta'ala, this spiritual and physical rectification will be a source of esteem for him in this world and a source of immense treasure for him upon his death when a person is in dire need of his good deeds. As for him who adopts anything contrary to this Taqwa, he would on that day, wish that there be a considerable distance between him and his evil deeds. And Allah cautions you about Himself (His punishment etc.) and (this caution is because) Allah is Most Kind to His servants.

The word of Allah is true. He executes His promises. There is no reneging on His promises because Allah Ta'ala declares: 'The word that emanates from Me cannot be altered'.

So fear Allah in your external and internal affairs and in the issues related to this world and the hereafter. 'He who adopts Taqwa, Allah will wipe out his sins and grant him an enormous reward. And he who adopts Taqwa has attained enormous success. Taqwa is something that thwarts the wrath, punishment and anger of Allah. The Taqwa of Allah will spiritually illuminate the faces on the day of judgement and it will be a source of acquiring the pleasure of Allah and a source of elevated ranks in the hereafter. Take your share (of this Taqwa) whatever you can manage and do not be lacking in the affairs of Allah.

Allah has revealed a book for your guidance and He has clarified His path to differentiate between the truthful and the liars. So, just as Allah has favoured you, you should also be favourable (in complying with His instructions, harbour enmity towards His enemies and implement Jihaad in His path.

Allah has chosen you and He has named you as Muslims (His obedient servants). The objective of Allah is that he who is to be destroyed will be destroyed even after clear evidence and he who is to live (as a believer) will live (with insight) after clear evidence.

There is no might and power besides Allah. Remember Allah abundantly and practice for the time after this day (hereafter). He who rectifies his affairs with Allah, Allah will suffice for him against the people and nobody will be able to harm him because the decree of Allah is executed upon the people and the will of the people is not implemented upon Allah. He is the exclusive master and owner of the people whilst the people do not own anything of Allah. He controls the people and they have no control whatsoever over Him.

Allah is the greatest. And there is no power and might save in the control of Allah, the most magnificent."

Upon the completion of Jumu'ah, Rasulullah ﷺ mounted his camel and set out in the direction of Madinah Munawwarah. He seated Hadhrat Abu Bakr رضى الله عنه directly behind him on the camel. A vast number of Ansaar, armed with their weaponry, were walking to his right, to his left and behind him.

We spent some time in this beautiful masjid, performing Salaatul Ishraaq and making dua to Allah Ta'ala. One's stay in Quba should remind one of the great incident of Hijrat. Sahaabah *(radiyallahu anhum ajmaeen)* left their homes, their families, their businesses and their wealth for the sake of Deen, for the sake of Allah Ta'ala, for the sake of His Nabi ﷺ. To leave one's home, family, belongings and surroundings only for the sake of Allah Ta'ala, for Islam and for Deen is the message Masjid-e-Quba gives to its visitors. When in Quba, stand up and make a firm intention to hand over ones life for Allah's Deen like the Sahaabah of Nabi Muhammad ﷺ had done. May Allah Ta'ala accept us all for His Deen and bless us with His special blessings.

CHAPTER Nine

Mount Uhud

After performing Ishraaq Salaah in Masjid-e-Quba, we continued towards the Mountain of Uhud. This is that area where some of the most valuable blood of this Ummah was spilled. This is that place where history will never again witness such loyalty, faithfulness and love. This is where the uncle of Rasulullah ﷺ, Hadhrat Hamzah ؓ was martyred, his limbs cut off and his liver chewed. This is that mountain from which Anas bin Nadhar ؓ perceived the fragrance of Jannah. It was here that he jumped into the thick of the enemy and sustained more than eighty wounds until he was eventually martyred. It was here that the mubaarak tooth of Rasulullah ﷺ was made shaheed. His mubaarak head was wounded at this very place. Uhud is that place where the pride of the youth of Makkah, Mus'ab bin Umair ؓ was buried with only one piece of cloth that could not cover his entire body. His feet had to be

Mount Uhud

covered with leaves and his head was covered with cloth. This is where Hadhrat Talhah ﷺ showed his love and allegiance to Rasulullah ﷺ and earned the special duas of the beloved Nabi ﷺ. He stood in front of our Nabi ﷺ and blocked the arrows with his hand thus preventing them from falling upon Nabi ﷺ until his hand became paralyzed. This is where Abu Dujaanah Al-Ansaari ﷺ stood like a human shield in front of Nabi ﷺ and protected him from the attack of the enemy.

When walking in the surroundings of Uhud, one is still able to perceive the sacrifices of these martyrs.

This mountain still calls out to its visitors the very same words that the illustrious Sahaabah *(radiyallahu anhum)* shouted out on that day

$$\text{مُوْتُوْا عَلٰى مَا مَاتَ عَلَيْهِ رَسُوْلُ اللهِ صَلَّى اللهُ عَلَيْهِ وَ سَلَّمْ}$$

Give your life for that cause which Rasulullah ﷺ had given his life.

This voice can still be heard up to this day with the ears of the heart. O visitor to Uhud, who is there to renew his pledge with Allah Ta'ala that my life, my wealth, my family, my honour and my prestige all be sacrificed for Allah Ta'ala, His Rasul ﷺ and His Deen?

As we drove towards the mountain of Uhud a sign board read the following words of Rasulullah ﷺ.

"This is a mountain which loves us and we love it."

How fortunate is this mountain? It has secured for itself the love of Allah's Nabi ﷺ. If only we could have been this mountain just so that we could hear these words from Rasulullah ﷺ that he loves us. O Allah, if a hard mountain of rock can secure for itself the love and muhabbat of Rasulullah ﷺ, bless our hard hearts also with his noble love.

May Allah Ta'ala, through His infinite Grace and Mercy, secure His special muhabbat (love) as well as the love of His beloved Nabi ﷺ for each and every Ummati. *Aameen*. If we have sincere muhabbat and love for Nabi ﷺ, *Insha Allah*, we will also enjoy the company of Rasulullah ﷺ and His noble Sahaabah (*radiyallahu anhum*).

We disembarked from the vehicle and walked slowly towards the graves of the Shuhadaa. First we conveyed salaams to Sayyidush Shuhadaa, Hadhrat Hamzah ibn Abdul Muttalib ؓ then to Hadhrat Mus'ab bin Umair ؓ, Hadhrat Hanzalah ؓ and the other seventy martyrs buried in Uhud. We made dua that Allah Ta'ala grant us a miniscule of the loyalty and spirit of sacrifice that these illustrious Sahaabah displayed.

Shaikhul Hadith, Hadhrat Moulana Muhammad Zakariyya Kandhlawi (*rahmatullahi alayh*) has advised the visitor to Madinah Shareef as follows:

"It is mustahab for the visitor to Madinah Munawwarah to visit the graves of the Shuhadaa (martyrs) of Uhud every Thursday. Perform Fajar Salaah in Masjidun Nabawi and then leave so that you may return before Zuhr and perform your salaah with jamaat in Masjidun Nabawi. Perhaps Thursday is chosen for this visit because it was on that day that this battle was fought. At Uhud, first go to the grave of Hadhrat Hamzah ؓ, the uncle of Rasulullah ﷺ, about whom Rasulullah

ﷺ has said: "The best of my uncles is Hamzah," and "On the day of Qiyaamah, Hamzah shall be the leader of the Shuhadaa." There the visitor should stand with humility and respect. Then go to the graves of the rest of those who passed away for the sake of Allah Ta'ala and Islam in the Battle of Uhud. As we stood on the plains of Uhud, the amazing scene of this fierce battle began playing in our minds.

The Battle

The following pages vividly describe the entire Battle of Uhud from the masterpiece, Seerat-e-Mustafa of Hadhrat Moulana Idrees Kandhlawi (rahmatullahi alayh).

After their defeat in Badar, the Quraish were burning from within and planned to avenge their defeat. They prepared an army of 3000 strong and left Makkah Mukarramah with great pomp and glory. Hadhrat 'Abbaas ؓ made a comprehensive note of these details and forwarded it to Rasulullah ﷺ with a high-speed messenger. The moment Rasulullah ﷺ received this intelligence, he despatched Anas ؓ and Munis ؓ to acquire additional information about the Quraysh. They returned and informed Rasulullah ﷺ that the Qurayshi army has almost reached Madinah. Thereafter, Rasulullah ﷺ sent Habbaab bin Munzir ؓ to determine the number of people in the army. He returned and provided an accurate estimate to Rasulullah ﷺ.

All night long, S'ad bin Mu'aaz ؓ, Usaid bin Hudhair ؓ and S'ad bin 'Ubaadah ؓ were on guard in Masjidun-Nabawi and soldiers on watch were posted all around the city as well.

Since Abdullah bin Ubayy, the chief of the hypocrites, was a talented and experienced man in such affairs, he was also consulted. He said: "Past experience will attest to the fact that whenever an enemy attacked Madinah and the residents of Madinah confronted the enemy within the boundaries of the city, the Madanis triumphed. On the contrary, whenever they challenged the enemy on the outside, they were defeated. O Rasulullah! Do not step out of the boundaries of the city. By Allah! Whenever we stepped out of Madinah we were subject to a great deal of suffering at the hands of the enemy and when the enemy launched an attack upon us whilst we took up a defensive position within the boundaries of Madinah, the enemy suffered a dreadful thrashing at our hands. Why don't you blockade and fortify the entire city and if, per chance, the enemy somehow manages to breach this blockade, the men will confront them with swords whilst the women and children will rain down showers of stones upon them. And if the enemy retreats disappointed without penetrating the city, our objective will be fulfilled."

Nonetheless, some of the senior Sahaabah رضي الله عنهم also joined the ranks of the younger Sahaabah رضي الله عنهم and insisted that the enemy be engaged out of the city of Madinah. They said: "O Rasulullah! We were eagerly expecting such a day and we begged Allah Ta'ala to show us this day soon. Now Allah Ta'ala has given us the chance and the journey is also a short one."

Hadhrat Hamzah رضي الله عنه, S'ad bin 'Ubaadah رضي الله عنه and Nu'maan bin Maalik رضي الله عنه said: "O Rasulullah صلى الله عليه وسلم! If we defend ourselves whilst holed up within the boundaries of the Madinah, our enemy will scornfully regard us as weak cowards in the path of Allah Ta'ala."

Hadhrat Hamzah رضي الله عنه said:

وَالَّذِيْ اَنْزَلَ عَلَيْكَ الْكِتَابَ لَا اَطْعَمُ الْيَوْمَ طَعَامًا حَتّٰى اُجَادِلَهُمْ بِسَيْفِيْ خَارِجَ الْمَدِيْنَةِ

"I swear by the Being Who has revealed the book upon you! I will not eat until I have engaged the enemy with my sword out of Madinah."

Nu'maan bin Maalik Ansaari رضى الله عنه said:

يَا رَسُوْلَ اللهِ لَا تَحْرِمْنَا الْجَنَّةَ، فَوَالَّذِيْ بَعَثَكَ بِالْحَقِّ لَاَدْخُلَنَّ الْجَنَّةَ

"O Rasulullah! We beg of you not to deprive us of this opportunity to enter Jannah. I swear by the Being Who has sent you with the truth! I will surely enter Jannah."

Rasulullah ﷺ asked: "On what grounds?" Nu'maan رضى الله عنه replied:

لِاَنِّيْ اَشْهَدُ اَنْ لَّا اِلٰهَ اِلَّا اللهُ وَاَنَّكَ رَسُوْلُ اللهِ وَلَا اَفِرُّ لِيَوْمِ الزَّحْفِ

"Owing to the fact that I testify that there is none worthy of worship but Allah and that you are His messenger and also due to the fact that I am not prone to flee from the battlefield."

According to another narration, he said:

لِاَنِّيْ اُحِبُّ اللهَ وَرَسُوْلَهُ

"Owing to the fact that I love Allah and His Rasool"

To this Rasulullah ﷺ remarked: "You have spoken the truth."

When Rasulullah ﷺ noticed the enthusiasm of the devotees of Jannah, i.e. the younger Sahaabah رضى الله عنهم, to fight out of Madinah and when he detected a similar passion for martyrdom from some of the senior Muhaajireen and Ansaar like Hadhrat Hamzah رضى الله عنه and S'ad bin 'Ubaadah رضى الله عنه, then Rasulullah ﷺ also elected to do the same.

This happened on Friday. After the Jumu'ah Salaah, Rasulullah ﷺ delivered a sermon in which he aroused their enthusiasm for Jihaad and charged them to prepare for battle.

The moment the sincere devotees, the dear lovers, the earnest worshippers and those who were keen to meet Allah Ta'ala heard this, it was as though a spark of life was infused within their souls and they deduced that the time had finally arrived for their liberation from the 'jail' of this world.

خُرم آن روز کزیں منزل ویران بَرَوم   راحتِ جان طلبم و زپے جانان بَرَوم

Blessed be the day when I am to depart from this desolate place; When I will be at ease in front of my beloved.

Raaf'i bin Khadeej رضى الله عنه was also amongst these youngsters who were presented to Rasulullah ﷺ. He was smart enough to stand on the tips of his toes to appear far taller than his age. Rasulullah ﷺ permitted him to join the army. It is also said that he was a well-skilled archer.

Samurah bin Jundub رضى الله عنه was one of the children who was refused by Rasulullah ﷺ. With an expression of deep sorrow, he lamented before his stepfather, Muri bin Sinaan رضى الله عنه: "O father! Raaf'i (who is my contemporary) is permitted to join the army whilst I get left behind? I am far stronger than him and I am certain that I will overpower him in wrestling."

Muri bin Sinaan ﺭﺿﻲﺍﻟﻠﻪﻋﻨﻪ went up to Rasulullah ﷺ and submitted: "O Rasulullah! You allowed Raaf'i to participate and sent my son Samurah back whereas Samurah will surely be able to wrestle him to the ground."

Rasulullah ﷺ then called on both the youngsters to match their capabilities in wrestling. When Samurah prevailed, Rasulullah ﷺ permitted him as well.

Young and old, child or adult, every single one of them was intoxicated with the spirit of sacrifice. Well before they were actually martyred, they were martyred by the sword of submission.

Return of the Hypocrites

As Rasulullah ﷺ got closer to Uhud, the chief of the hypocrites, Abdullah bin Ubayy bin Salool, who came with a group of 300, decided to turn back saying: "You disregarded my advice. Why should we now throw ourselves into danger needlessly? This is certainly not a war. If we believed this to be war, we would have unquestionably joined you."

In regards to such people, the following verses were revealed:

وَلِيَعْلَمَ الَّذِيْنَ نَافَقُوْا ۚ وَقِيْلَ لَهُمْ تَعَالَوْا قَاتِلُوْا فِيْ سَبِيْلِ اللهِ اَوِ ادْفَعُوْا ۗ قَالُوْا لَوْ نَعْلَمُ قِتَالًا لَّا اتَّبَعْنٰكُمْ ۗ هُمْ لِلْكُفْرِ يَوْمَئِذٍ اَقْرَبُ مِنْهُمْ لِلْاِيْمَانِ ۚ يَقُوْلُوْنَ بِاَفْوَاهِهِمْ مَّا لَيْسَ فِيْ قُلُوْبِهِمْ ۗ وَاللهُ اَعْلَمُ بِمَا يَكْتُمُوْنَ ۞

"And that He may test the hypocrites, it was said to them: 'Come, fight in the path of Allah or (at least) defend (yourselves)'. They replied: 'Had we known that there was a genuine fight, we would certainly have followed you.' They were that day, closer to disbelief than to Imaan, saying with their mouths that which was not in their hearts. And Allah is most knowledgeable of that which they conceal."

[Surah Aali-'Imraan verse 167]

Subsequently only 700 Sahaabah ﷢ were left with Rasulullah ﷺ, of which only 100 were dressed in body armour. The whole army had just two horses; one for Rasulullah ﷺ and the other belonged to Abu Burdah bin Niyaar Haarisi ﷠.

Drawing up the Battle Lines

Subsequent to the performance of his Salaah, Rasulullah ﷺ directed his attention towards the army. Facing Madinah with Uhud behind him, Rasulullah ﷺ drew up the battle lines. These columns of saintly souls who prior to this were standing humbly before Allah Ta'ala were now standing to sacrifice their lives in His path of Jihaad.

Baraa bin 'Aazib ﷠ narrates: "Rasulullah ﷺ positioned a division of fifty archers at the back of Mount Uhud to prevent any attack by the Quraysh from this direction. He appointed Abdullah bin Jubair ﷠ as their commander and sternly warned them: 'Do not move from this point even if you notice us prevailing over the disbelievers and even if you catch sight of the disbelievers overpowering us, do not ever abandon your positions and do not come to assist us.'

Rasulullah ﷺ forewarned them: "Even if you catch sight of us being picked apart by birds, then too do not move from this position. Remain here and protect us from the rear and even if you witness us being massacred, do not leave your positions to assist us. If you happen to see us gathering the war booty, then too stay where you are and do not dare join us."

Abu Dujaanah ؓ takes the sword of Rasulullah ﷺ

As the opposing parties drew their battle lines, Rasulullah ﷺ, grasping a sword in his hand, addressed the Sahaabah ؓ and asked:

"Who will take this sword with its due right?"

On hearing this, a number of hands reached out to acquire this noble boon but Rasulullah ﷺ held back. In the meantime, Abu Dujaanah ؓ stepped ahead and asked: "What is the right of this sword, O Rasulullah?" Rasulullah ﷺ replied: "The right of this sword is that it be used to strike the enemies of Allah until they are defeated."

According to another narration, Rasulullah ﷺ said: "The right of this sword is that it is not to be used to kill a Muslim and that a person does not take flight when engaging the disbelievers with this sword."

Abu Dujaanah ؓ said: "O Rasulullah! I will take this sword with its due right." In other words, "I will endeavour to fulfil its right."

Rasulullah ﷺ promptly handed over the sword to Abu Dujaanah رضي الله عنه.

Abu Dujaanah رضي الله عنه was a gallant, dauntless and brave warrior. During the heat of battle, he would take on a distinctive parade and be overwhelmed with an extraordinary degree of arduous passion. Whilst engaging the enemy, he would don a red 'Imaamah (turban) and stride with a charming grace. Perhaps this is why Rasulullah ﷺ handed the sword over to him as evidenced by his future skills as a warrior.

The Battle Begins

From the side of the Quraysh, the first person to stride onto the battlefield was Abu 'Aamir who was the leader of the Aws tribe (of Madinah) during the pre-Islamic times of ignorance and due to his devoutness and religiousness, was famously known as Raahib (the pope). When the glow of Islam radiated in Madinah, he was unable to stomach this and left Madinah to settle down in Makkah. Instead of Raahib, Rasulullah ﷺ named him Faasiq (criminal).

This Faasiq came to Makkah and inflamed the Quraysh to take up arms against Rasulullah ﷺ and he himself joined the Quraysh in this campaign of Uhud. He led them to believe that when the people of Aws catch sight of him, they would willingly desert Rasulullah ﷺ and join forces with him.

The first contestant

In the frontline of Uhud, this same Abu 'Aamir, stepped out as the first challenger and as he swaggered onto the battlefield, he bellowed:

"O people of Aws! I am Abu 'Aamir."

May Allah Ta'ala cool the eyes of the Aws tribe, who promptly responded:

"O Faasiq! May Allah never cool your eyes."

On hearing this humiliating response, Abu 'Aamir rapidly retreated, unsuccessful in his endeavours and exclaimed: "After I left them, my people have turned for the worse."

The second contestant:

He was followed onto the battlefield by the flag-bearer of the disbelievers, Talhah bin Abi Talhah and with an air of arrogance, he challenged:

"O companions of Muhammad! You believe that Allah Ta'ala would promptly despatch us into hell with the aid of your swords whilst He would swiftly admit you with the aid of our swords into paradise. So, is there anyone from amongst you who would like to be swiftly admitted into paradise with my sword or whose sword would promptly dispatch me to hell?"

On hearing this, Hadhrat Ali رَضِيَ اللهُ عَنْهُ strode forth and engaged him in a swordfight. Hadhrat Ali رَضِيَ اللهُ عَنْهُ delivered a slicing blow to his leg and he fell face down to the ground exposing his satar (private area). Overcome with shame, Hadhrat Ali رَضِيَ اللهُ عَنْهُ stepped back. Rasulullah صَلَّى اللهُ عَلَيْهِ وَسَلَّمَ asked: "O Ali! What made you withdraw?" He replied: "At the uncovering of his satar, I was overcome with shame."

Hadhrat Ali رَضِيَ اللهُ عَنْهُ then smote him on his head so severely that his head split into two.

This delighted Rasulullah صَلَّى اللهُ عَلَيْهِ وَسَلَّمَ and he exclaimed: "Allahu Akbar!" The Muslims also chanted exclamations of Allahu Akbar!

The third contestant:

Thereafter, 'Usmaan bin Abi Talhah, grasping the flag of the disbelievers, stepped forth onto the battlefield, reciting the following inflammatory stanza:

> "It is an obligation upon the flag-bearer to ensure that his spear is tinted with the blood of the enemy or it breaks into pieces."

In response, Hadhrat Hamzah رَضِيَ اللَّهُ عَنْهُ strode up and attacked him, severing both his arms at the shoulders. The flag fell and in an instant he was no more.

The fourth contestant:

Thereafter, the flag was taken up by Abu S'ad bin Abi Talhah. S'ad bin Abi Waqqaas رَضِيَ اللَّهُ عَنْهُ discharged an arrow towards him. It pierced his neck with such force that his tongue was pushed out of his mouth. S'ad bin Abi Waqqaas رَضِيَ اللَّهُ عَنْهُ then promptly finished him off.

The fifth contestant:

Thereafter the flag was taken up by Musaf'i bin Talhah bin Abi Talhah. With just one blow, Hadhrat 'Aasim bin Saabit رَضِيَ اللَّهُ عَنْهُ put him to death.

The sixth contestant:

The flag was then hoisted by Haaris bin Talhah bin Abi Talhah. He too was finished off with just one blow by Hadhrat 'Aasim bin Saabit رَضِيَ اللَّهُ عَنْهُ.

The seventh contestant:

Kilaab bin Talhah bin Abi Talhah then stepped out with the flag. Hadhrat Zubair رَضِيَ اللَّهُ عَنْهُ stepped ahead and did away with him.

The eighth contestant:

Thereafter the flag was taken up by Julaas bin Talhah bin Abi Talhah. The moment he stepped out, Hadhrat Talhah رَضِيَ اللَّهُ عَنْهُ finished him off.

The ninth contestant:

The flag was then taken up by Artaat Shurahbil. Hadhrat Ali رَضِيَ اللَّهُ عَنْهُ swiftly eliminated him.

The tenth contestant:

Shuraih bin Qaariz then took up the flag and strode out. He too was instantaneously finished off. The killer of Shuraih could not be ascertained.

The eleventh contestant:

Therafter, their slave by the name of Suwaab stepped out holding the flag. Either Hadhrat S'ad bin Abi Waqqaas رَضِيَ اللَّهُ عَنْهُ or Hadhrat Hamzah رَضِيَ اللَّهُ عَنْهُ or Hadhrat Ali رَضِيَ اللَّهُ عَنْهُ – according to conflicting narrations – finished him off too.

In this manner, twenty-two chieftains of the Quraysh were eliminated.

The Valour of Abu Dujaanah ﷺ

Abu Dujaanah ﷺ, to whom Rasulullah ﷺ conferred his blessed sword, was a dauntless and gallant warrior. Firstly, he produced a red 'Imaamah (turban) and tied it onto his head. He then paraded onto the battlefield reciting the following stanzas:

اَنَا الَّذِيْ عَاهَدَنِيْ خَلِيْلِيْ   وَنَحْنُ بِالسَّفْحِ لَدَى النَّخِيْلِ

"I am the one from whom my Khalil (beloved whose love has penetrated every fibre of my being, i.e. Rasulullah ﷺ) had taken a pledge whilst we were at the foot of the mountain close to the date orchard.

اَنْ لَّا اَقُوْمَ الدَّهْرَ فِي الْكُيُوْلِ   اَضْرِبُ بِسَيْفِ اللهِ وَالرَّسُوْلِ

The pledge was that I would never stand within the ranks of the rear and I would continue engaging the enemy with the sword of Allah and His Rasool."

When Rasulullah ﷺ caught sight of Abu Dujaanah ﷺ swaggering in this manner he commented: "Allah abhors such a gait except on such occasions."

In other words, when engaging the enemy, this (pride) is for the sake of Allah Ta'ala and His Rasool ﷺ and not for selfish reasons of pride and arrogance.

Tearing through the ranks of the enemy, whoever Abu Dujaanah ﷺ came across would fall dead to the ground. He ploughed ahead until Hindah, the wife of Abu Sufyaan, confronted him. Abu Dujaanah ﷺ raised his sword to strike her but restrained himself thinking that it was unbecoming of him to use Rasulullah's ﷺ sword against a woman.

According to another narration, when Abu Dujaanah رضي الله عنه drew close to Hindah, she screeched for help but nobody came to her assistance. Abu Dujaanah رضي الله عنه says: "At that time I felt it rather indecent to test the sword of Rasulullah ﷺ on a vulnerable and helpless woman."

Valour and Martyrdom of Hadhrat Hamzah رضي الله عنه

The dauntless array of attacks launched by Hadhrat Hamzah رضي الله عنه subdued the disbelievers into a state of overwhelming panic. The instant he raised his sword upon anyone, the next instant the enemy would fall to the ground.

Wahshi bin Harb was the slave of Jubair bin Mut'im. During the Battle of Badr, Jubair's uncle Tu'aymah bin 'Adi was slain by Hadhrat Hamzah رضي الله عنه. Jubair was heartbroken at the death of his uncle. Jubair promised Wahshi that if he killed Hamzah *(radiyallahu anhu)* in revenge for his uncle, he would set him free. When the Quraysh set out for the battle of Uhud, Wahshi also accompanied them.

As the opposing parties formed their ranks at Uhud and the battle got underway, Sib'a bin 'Abdul-'Uzza swaggered onto the battlefield yelling: "Is there anyone who dares to challenge me?"

Heading up towards him, Hadhrat Hamzah رضي الله عنه replied: "O Sib'a! O son of the woman who specialises in female circumcision! How dare you brazenly defy Allah and His Rasool?" Saying this, Hadhrat Hamzah رضي الله عنه attacked him with his sword and in just a single thrust, he promptly despatched him to his death.

Meanwhile, Wahshi hid himself behind a boulder lying in ambush for Hadhrat Hamzah ﺭﺿﻰﺍﻟﻠﻪﻋﻨﻪ. The moment Hadhrat Hamzah ﺭﺿﻰﺍﻟﻠﻪﻋﻨﻪ passed by, he struck him on his back with such force that his spear penetrated through his abdomen emerging at his navel. Hadhrat Hamzah ﺭﺿﻰﺍﻟﻠﻪﻋﻨﻪ managed tottering a few steps but eventually succumbed to his injury and 'drank from the cup of martyrdom'.

Martyrdom of Hadhrat Hanzalah ﺭﺿﻰﺍﻟﻠﻪﻋﻨﻪ

Hadhrat Hanzalah ﺭﺿﻰﺍﻟﻠﻪﻋﻨﻪ also accompanied Rasulullah ﺻﻠﻰﺍﻟﻠﻪﻋﻠﻴﻪﻭﺳﻠﻢ on this campaign.

Abu Sufyaan and Hadhrat Hanzalah ﺭﺿﻰﺍﻟﻠﻪﻋﻨﻪ clashed with one another in a fierce swordfight. Hadhrat Hanzalah ﺭﺿﻰﺍﻟﻠﻪﻋﻨﻪ sprang forward to strike Abu Sufyaan but Shaddaad bin Aws fatally attacked him from the rear rendering him a Shaheed.

On this occasion, Rasulullah ﺻﻠﻰﺍﻟﻠﻪﻋﻠﻴﻪﻭﺳﻠﻢ remarked: "I witnessed the angels bathing Hanzalah ﺭﺿﻰﺍﻟﻠﻪﻋﻨﻪ with pure hail water from silver goblets."

Upon enquiry from his wife, it was learnt that he had set out for Jihaad in the state of Janaabat and he was martyred in this state.

The wife of Hadhrat Hanzalah ﺭﺿﻰﺍﻟﻠﻪﻋﻨﻪ saw a dream the night preceding his martydom that a door had opened from the heavens and Hadhrat Hanzalah ﺭﺿﻰﺍﻟﻠﻪﻋﻨﻪ had entered there. As soon as he entered, the door closed. His wife understood from this dream that Hanzalah ﺭﺿﻰﺍﻟﻠﻪﻋﻨﻪ was about to leave this world.

On the termination of the battle, water was seen dripping from his body. This is why he was eminently known as Ghaseelul-Malaa'ikah (the one bathed by the angels).

Since Hanzalah's ﷺ father Abu 'Aamir was fighting against Rasulullah ﷺ, Hadhrat Hanzalah ﷺ sought Rasulullah's ﷺ permission to assassinate his own father but Rasulullah ﷺ prohibited him.

These dauntless assaults and valiant attacks of the Muslims brought the Quraysh to their knees on the battlefield leaving them turning their backs and hurrying about for cover. Struck with chilling anxiety, the ladies also fled towards the mountains whilst the Muslims busied themselves in amassing the war-booty.

Muslims Archers abandon their positions

When the group of archers who were appointed to guard the rear mountain pass noticed the victory of the Muslims and their subsequent amassing of the war booty, they also decided to abandon their positions and dash forth. Their Ameer Abdullah bin Jubair ﷺ repeatedly pleaded with them not to abandon their positions and reminded them about Rasulullah's ﷺ emphatic order not to leave their positions under any circumstances whatsoever. However, these people refused to take heed and they deserted their positions and proceeded to collect the booty.

Martyrdom of Abdullah bin Jubair ﷺ

Thus only Abdullah bin Jubair ﷺ and ten companions were left at this strategic position. Since the Muslims failed to comply with the wishes of Rasulullah ﷺ, the victory swiftly turned into defeat. When Khaalid bin Waleed, who was with the right flank of the Mushrikeen, caught sight of the vulnerable pass, he attacked from the rear. This attack rendered Abdullah bin Jubair رَضِىَٱللَّهُعَنْهُ and ten of his companions as martyrs.

Martyrdom of Mus'ab bin 'Umair رَضِىَٱللَّهُعَنْهُ

This surprisingly sudden and unexpected attack by the disbelievers left the ranks of the Muslims in bewilderment and the enemy managed to draw threateningly close to Rasulullah ﷺ.

The flag-bearer of the Muslims, Mus'ab bin 'Umair رَضِىَٱللَّهُعَنْهُ was standing close to Rasulullah ﷺ. He valiantly tackled the disbelievers in the defence of Rasulullah ﷺ until he himself was martyred. Thereafter, Rasulullah ﷺ consigned the flag to Hadhrat Ali رَضِىَٱللَّهُعَنْهُ.

Since Mus'ab bin 'Umair رَضِىَٱللَّهُعَنْهُ closely resembled Rasulullah ﷺ, a certain shaytaan circulated a rumour that Rasulullah ﷺ, the target of the disbelievers, was martyred. Immediately, a gloomy mood of bewilderment and apprehension spread throughout the muslim ranks. The moment they heard this heart rendering news, they lost their senses and fell into a state of panic. In this state of panic, they were unable to differentiate between friend and foe and they started attacking one another.

The father of Hadhrat Huzayfah رَضِىَٱللَّهُعَنْهُ is erroneously martyred

Hadhrat Huzayfah's رَضِىَٱللَّهُعَنْهُ father Yamaan رَضِىَٱللَّهُعَنْهُ, was also caught up in this state of chaos. From a distance, Huzayfah رَضِىَٱللَّهُعَنْهُ caught sight of his father coming under attack from the Muslims. He yelled at them: "O servants of Allah! That is my father." However, who could have heard him in this state of utter chaos and they eventually killed him. When the Muslims learnt that they erroneously killed Huzayfah's ﷺ father, they were dreadfully ashamed and in a tone of downright remorse said: "By Allah, we failed to recognise him."

Hadhrat Huzayfah ﷺ remarked:

يَغْفِرُ اللّٰهُ لَكُمْ وَهُوَ اَرْحَمُ الرّٰحِمِيْنَ

"May Allah forgive you. He is the most merciful of those who show mercy."

Rasulullah ﷺ offered to pay him the Diyat (blood money) in compensation but Hadhrat Huzayfah ﷺ declined to accept it. This further enhanced Huzayfah's ﷺ esteem in the eyes of Rasulullah ﷺ.

The unexpected attack of Khaalid bin Waleed

Although a great many brave souls were left struggling on the battlefield following the unanticipated attack of Khaalid bin Waleed, nothing could shake the steadfastness and perseverance of Rasulullah ﷺ. How could anything agitate his steadfastness because the Nabi of Allah can never be, Allah forbid, a coward. The mountains may move but the messengers of Allah Ta'ala will surely stand their ground. The valour of a single Nabi far outweighs the valour of the entire world of champions.

Describing this scene, Hadhrat Miqdaad ﷺ says:

"I swear by the celestial being Who sent Rasulullah ﷺ with the truth, Rasulullah's ﷺ feet did not budge an inch in his resolute stance against the disbelievers. A group of the Sahaabah ﷺ would sometimes come to his assistance and sometimes they would disperse and quite often I witnessed Rasulullah ﷺ discharging arrows and hurling stones at the disbelievers until the enemy melted away."

Bodyguards of Rasulullah ﷺ

During this state of turmoil, fourteen Sahaabah رضي الله عنهم stood their ground with Rasulullah ﷺ; seven from the Muhaajireen and seven from the Ansaar. They were:

Muhaajireen	Ansaar
1. Abu Bakr رضي الله عنه	1. Abu Dujaanah رضي الله عنه
2. 'Umar bin Khattaab رضي الله عنه	2. Habbaab bin Munzir رضي الله عنه
3. 'Abdur-Rahmaan bin 'Awf رضي الله عنه	3. 'Aasim bin Saabit رضي الله عنه
4. S'ad bin Abi Waqqaas رضي الله عنه	4. Haaris bin Simmah رضي الله عنه
5. Talhah رضي الله عنه	5. Suhail bin Hunaif رضي الله عنه
6. Zubair bin 'Awwam رضي الله عنه	6. S'ad bin Mu'aaz رضي الله عنه
7. Abu 'Ubaidah رضي الله عنه	7. Usaid bin Hudhair رضي الله عنه

Hadhrat Ali's رضي الله عنه name was not mentioned in the Muhaajireen because following the martyrdom of Mus'ab bin 'Umair رضي الله عنه, Rasulullah ﷺ appointed him the flag bearer of the Muslim army. He was engaged in fighting the enemy.

These fourteen gallant personalities were constantly with Rasulullah ﷺ. Occasionally when the need arose some of them would go away but swiftly return. This is why Rasulullah ﷺ was sometimes left with twelve people.

Unexpected attack of the Quraysh against Rasulullah ﷺ

When the Quraysh launched an attack on Rasulullah ﷺ, he invited: "Who will rid these people of me and render himself my companion in Jannah?" Hadhrat Anas ؓ says: "There were seven Ansaar with Rasulullah ﷺ and every one of them fought valiantly until, one by one, they were all made Shaheed."

Rasulullah ﷺ invited:

"Is there any man who is prepared to sell his life for us?"

Immediately upon hearing this, Ziyaad bin Sakan ؓ and five other Ansaar responded to his call. One after the other, each one of them demonstrated their spirit of sacrifice until they were all rendered Shaheed. They bartered their lives in exchange for Jannah.

Martyrdom of Ziyaad bin Sakan ؓ

Ziyaad ؓ was blessed with an additional privilege. When he fell wounded to the ground, Rasulullah ﷺ said: "Bring him closer to me."

When his companions brought him to Rasulullah ﷺ, Ziyaad ؓ placed his cheek on the blessed foot of Rasulullah ﷺ and consigned his life over to Allah Ta'ala. إنا لله وإنا إليه راجعون.

Attack of 'Utbah bin Abi Waqqaas upon Rasulullah ﷺ

Availing himself of an opportune moment, 'Utbah bin Abi Waqqaas, the brother of S'ad bin Abi Waqqaas ؓ hurled a stone upon Rasulullah ﷺ with such force that Rasulullah ﷺ lost a lower tooth and his lower lip was injured. S'ad bin Abi Waqqaas ؓ says: "I was not as eager to kill anyone else as much as I was eager to kill my brother 'Utbah bin Abi Waqqaas."

Attack of Abdullah bin Qami-ah upon Rasulullah ﷺ

Abdullah bin Qami-ah, a celebrated wrestler of the Quraysh, attacked Rasulullah ﷺ with such force that two links of his armoured helmet pierced his cheek. Meanwhile, Abdullah bin Shihaab Zuhri hurled a stone at Rasulullah ﷺ injuring his blessed forehead. When his blessed face started bleeding, Abu Sa'eed Khudri's ؓ father, Maalik bin Sinaan ؓ sucked the blood and cleaned his blessed face. Rasulullah ﷺ promised: "The fire of Jahannam will never strike you."

Abu Umaamah ؓ relates: "After inflicting this injury to Rasulullah ﷺ, Ibn Qami-ah taunted:

خُذْهَا وَاَنَا اِبْنُ قَمِئَهْ

'Here, take it! I am the son of Qam-iah.'"

Rasulullah ﷺ replied:

اَقْمَاكَ اللّٰهُ

"May Allah disgrace and destroy you"

Barely a few days later, Allah Ta'ala set a mountain goat over him that tore him to pieces with its horns.

Support of Hadhrat Talhah رَضِىَ اللّٰهُ عَنْهُ to Rasulullah صَلَّى اللّٰهُ عَلَيْهِ وَسَلَّمَ

Since Rasulullah ﷺ was also donning a pair of heavy steel armour, he fell into a hole dug by 'Abu 'Amir, the Faasiq, for the Muslims. Hadhrat Ali رَضِىَ اللّٰهُ عَنْهُ held his hand and Hadhrat Talhah رَضِىَ اللّٰهُ عَنْهُ supported his waist and only then did he manage to stand upright.

On this occasion, he remarked: "If you wish to see a living martyr walking the surface of this earth, take a look at Talhah."

Hadhrat Aaishah رَضِىَ اللّٰهُ عَنْهَا narrates from her father Hadhrat Abu Bakr رَضِىَ اللّٰهُ عَنْهُ that when two links of the armoured helmet embedded themselves into the cheeks of Rasulullah ﷺ, Hadhrat Abu 'Ubaidah bin Jarrah رَضِىَ اللّٰهُ عَنْهُ gripped them with his teeth and plucked them out. He lost two of his teeth in the process.

When Rasulullah ﷺ attempted to ascend one of the peaks of the mountain, his fatigue and weakness compounded by the burden of his double armour left him helpless. Hadhrat Talhah رَضِىَ اللّٰهُ عَنْهُ positioned himself in submission before Rasulullah ﷺ. Placing his foot on Talhah رَضِىَ اللّٰهُ عَنْهُ, Rasulullah ﷺ managed to climb up.

Hadhrat Zubair رَضِىَ اللّٰهُ عَنْهُ narrates: "On this occasion, I heard Rasulullah ﷺ declaring:

اَوْ جَبَ طَلْحَةُ

'Talhah has made Jannah compulsory for himself.'"

Qays bin Abi Haazim says: "I saw the hand of Talhah رَضِىَ اللهُ عَنْهُ that he used as a shield in defending Rasulullah ﷺ on the day of Uhud. His hand was completely paralysed."

On that day Hadhrat Talhah رَضِىَ اللهُ عَنْهُ sustained thirty-five or thirty-nine wounds to his body.

Hadhrat Aaishah رَضِىَ اللهُ عَنْهَا narrates that whenever Hadhrat Abu Bakr رَضِىَ اللهُ عَنْهُ mentioned the battle of Uhud, he would say:

كَانَ ذٰلِكَ الْيَوْمُ كُلُّهُ لِطَلْحَةَ

"That day was exclusively for Talhah."

Hadhrat Jaabir رَضِىَ اللهُ عَنْهُ narrates: "Whilst deflecting the attacks of the enemy, Hadhrat Talhah's رَضِىَ اللهُ عَنْهُ fingers were severed. Impulsively he cried out: 'Hassan.' Upon this Rasulullah ﷺ remarked:

'If you uttered Bismillah instead of Hassan, the angels would have raised you high up where the people would have been able to catch sight of you until they enter the atmosphere of the sky with you.'"

Hadhrat Aaishah رَضِىَ اللهُ عَنْهَا narrates from Hadhrat Abu Bakr رَضِىَ اللهُ عَنْهُ who says: "On the day of Uhud, we counted more than seventy wounds on the body of Talhah رَضِىَ اللهُ عَنْهُ."

Hadhrat Anas's رَضِىَ اللهُ عَنْهُ stepfather Hadhrat Abu Talhah رَضِىَ اللهُ عَنْهُ was protecting Rasulullah ﷺ with a shield. He was a master archer. On that day, he broke two or three bows. Whoever happened to pass by with a quiver of arrows, Rasulullah ﷺ would say: "Go and empty out your quiver before Abu Talhah."

Whenever Rasulullah ﷺ planned to watch over the people, Abu Talhah رضي الله عنه would plead with him:

> "May my parents be sacrificed for you, O Rasulullah ﷺ! Do not look over. An arrow of the enemy may strike you. Rather it strikes my chest instead of yours."

S'ad bin Abi Waqqaas رضي الله عنه too was a professional archer. On the day of Uhud, Rasulullah ﷺ pulled out all his arrows from his quiver and placed them before S'ad رضي الله عنه and said:

اِرْمِ فِدَاكَ اَبِيْ وَاُمِّيْ

"Go on, shoot the arrows. May my parents be sacrificed for you."

Hadhrat Ali رضي الله عنه narrates: "I have not heard Rasulullah ﷺ saying 'may my parents be sacrificed for you' for anyone other than S'ad bin Abi Waqqaas رضي الله عنه."

On the day of Uhud, Hadhrat S'ad رضي الله عنه fired one thousand arrows.

The Gallant Sacrifice of Abu Dujaanah رضي الله عنه

Abu Dujaanah رضي الله عنه positioned himself before Rasulullah ﷺ as a human shield with his back facing the enemy. Scores of arrows landed on his back but for fear of an arrow wounding Rasulullah ﷺ, Abu Dujaanah رضي الله عنه did not move an inch.

Rasulullah's ﷺ lamenting over the disbelievers

Hadhrat Anas ؓ narrates: "On the day of Uhud, Rasulullah ﷺ would continue wiping the blood off his blessed face and lament in the following words: 'How can a people who stained the face of their Nabi with blood ever be successful whilst the Nabi is merely inviting them towards their Rabb?'"

Rasulullah's ﷺ cursing the Qurayshi Chieftains

Hadhrat Saalim ؓ narrates that Rasulullah ﷺ cursed Safwaan bin Umayyah, Suhail bin 'Amr and Haaris bin Hishaam. Upon this, Allah Ta'ala revealed the following verse:

لَيْسَ لَكَ مِنَ الْاَمْرِ شَيْءٌ اَوْ يَتُوْبَ عَلَيْهِمْ اَوْ يُعَذِّبَهُمْ فَاِنَّهُمْ ظٰلِمُوْنَ ۝

"The decision is not for you to make (O Muhammad ﷺ, but for Allah alone). He may pardon them or He may punish them because they are sinners." [Surah Aali-'Imraan verse 128]

Hafiz Asqalaani *(rahmatullahi alayh)* says: "All three of them embraced Islam at the conquest of Makkah. Perhaps this is why Allah Ta'ala forbade Rasulullah ﷺ from cursing them and revealed the above aayat."

Hadhrat Abdullah bin Mas'ood ؓ says: "I can still distinctly visualise the scene where Rasulullah ﷺ was busy wiping the blood off his face and pleading with Allah:

رَبِّ اغْفِرْ لِقَوْمِيْ فَاِنَّهُمْ لَا يَعْلَمُوْنَ

Mount Uhud

"O my Rabb! Forgive my people because they do not know."

Qataadah bin Nu'maan رَضِيَ اللَّهُ عَنْهُ loses an eye

Qataadah bin Nu'maan رَضِيَ اللَّهُ عَنْهُ narrates: "On the day of Uhud, I positioned myself right in front of Rasulullah's ﷺ face and directed my face towards the enemy so that my face may bear the brunt of the arrows instead of the blessed face of Rasulullah ﷺ. One of the last arrows of the enemy landed with such force on my face that my eyeball sprung out. Holding it in my hand, I turned towards Rasulullah ﷺ. When he caught sight of my eye, his eyes welled up with tears and he made dua for me: 'O Allah! Just as Qataadah protected the face of your Nabi, protect his face and restore his eye to a condition better and sharper than what it was.' Saying this, Rasulullah ﷺ took the eyeball and replaced it into its socket. Instantaneously, my eyesight was restored. In fact, my eyesight turned out to be better and sharper than what it originally was."

According to another narration, Qataadah رَضِيَ اللَّهُ عَنْهُ held the eyeball in his hand and appeared before Rasulullah ﷺ, who said: "If you exercise patience, you will be rewarded with Jannah and if you wish I will replace your eyeball in its original position and make dua for you." Qataadah رَضِيَ اللَّهُ عَنْهُ replied: "O Rasulullah! I have a wife whom I love dearly. I fear that if I am left with one eye she may find it revolting and she may develop feelings of dislike and hatred towards me."

Taking hold of the eye, Rasulullah ﷺ replaced it into its socket and made the following dua: "O Allah! Grant him beauty and handsomeness."

Rumour of Rasulullah's ﷺ Martyrdom

When a false rumour of Rasulullah's ﷺ assassination began circulating, some Muslims lost courage. Despondently they said: "Since Rasulullah ﷺ is martyred, what is the need for fighting now?"

To this, Hadhrat Anas's رضى الله عنه paternal uncle countered: "O people! Muhammad ﷺ may have been killed but the Rabb of Muhammad ﷺ has not been killed. Continue fighting for whatever cause you had been fighting previously and sacrifice your lives for the same. What would you stay alive and do after the demise of Rasulullah ﷺ?"

Saying this, he stationed himself in the ranks of the enemy and fought them until he was martyred.

Martyrdom of Anas bin Nadr رضى الله عنه

Hadhrat Anas رضى الله عنه narrates: "My paternal uncle Anas bin Nadr رضى الله عنه was profoundly distressed for failing to take part in the battle of Badr. Once, he mentioned to Rasulullah ﷺ: 'O Rasulullah ﷺ! How lamentable that I could not participate in the foremost battle of Islam against the disbelievers. If Allah Ta'ala grants me the ability to participate in another Jihaad in the future, Allah will witness my gallant efforts and my heroic spirit of sacrifice.'"

During the battle of Uhud, when some people fled in defeat, Anas bin Nadr رضى الله عنه submitted before Allah Ta'ala: "O Allah! I beg your forgiveness from what some of the Muslims have done – fleeing from the battlefield - and I isolate myself from what the disbelievers have done."

Saying this, he advanced towards the enemy with a sword in his hand. When he caught sight of S'ad bin Mu'aaz ﷺ before him, he said:

$$\text{اَيْنَ يَا سَعْدُ اِنِّي اَجِدُ رِيْحَ الْجَنَّةِ دُوْنَ اُحُدٍ}$$

"Where to O S'ad?! I perceive the fragrance of Jannah by Uhud"

"Ah! I can smell the fragrance of Jannah emanating from the mountain of Uhud." Hadhrat Anas ﷺ strode forth and engaged the enemy until he was martyred. More than eighty wounds inflicted by swords and arrows were found on his body. Regarding him, the following verse was revealed:

$$\text{مِنَ الْمُؤْمِنِيْنَ رِجَالٌ صَدَقُوْا مَا عَاهَدُوا اللهَ عَلَيْهِ}$$

"Amongst the believers are men who have been true to their promise with Allah." [Surah Ahzaab verse 23]

The chief reason for the anguish facing the Muslims on this occasion was that they were unable to catch sight of Rasulullah ﷺ. The first person to recognise Rasulullah ﷺ during this upheaval was Ka'b bin Maalik ﷺ. Rasulullah ﷺ was wearing a helmet that was concealing his blessed face. Ka'b ﷺ says: "I recognised Rasulullah ﷺ from his radiant eyes. The moment I caught sight of him, I yelled: 'O Muslims! Glad tidings for you. There is Rasulullah ﷺ over there.'" Raising his hand to his face, Rasulullah ﷺ signalled him to maintain silence. Although Rasulullah ﷺ forbade him to mention this a second time, their hearts and minds were focused in that direction. This is why, following the single cheerful announcement of

Ka'b ﷺ, a few Muslims rushed off towards Rasulullah ﷺ like moths to a flame. Ka'b ﷺ says: "Thereafter Rasulullah ﷺ gave me his armour to wear whilst he wore my armour. Thinking that I am Rasulullah ﷺ, the enemy started letting loose a torrent of arrows upon me. I sustained more than twenty wounds on this occasion."

As a few Muslims gathered around Rasulullah ﷺ, he set off for the mountain pass. Amongst others, accompanying him were Abu Bakr, 'Umar, Ali, Talhah and Haaris bin Simmah ﷺ. Rasulullah ﷺ attempted to climb the mountain but due to weakness, exhaustion and the weight of the double armour, he was unable to climb up. This is why Hadhrat Talhah ﷺ sat down before him. Placing his foot on Talhah ﷺ, Rasulullah ﷺ climbed over with difficulty.

Killing of Ubayy bin Khalaf

In the meantime, Ubayy bin Khalaf came galloping on his horse, a horse that he fed and fattened with the sole intention of killing Rasulullah ﷺ.

When Rasulullah ﷺ got wind of his intentions, he at once said: "*Insha Allah*, I will kill him."

As he drew closer to the Muslims, the Sahaabah ﷺ sought Rasulullah's ﷺ permission to finish him off. Rasulullah ﷺ said: "Leave him. Allow him to get closer."

As he came up to them, Rasulullah ﷺ took a spear from Haaris bin Simmah ﷺ and inflicted a slight spear-jab to his neck. He started shrieking at the top of his voice and returned to his people bellowing: "By Allah! Muhammad has killed me."

His people attempted to console him saying: "It is nothing but a slight prick. It is not such a serious wound that you have to scream like this." Ubayy retorted: "Don't you know? Muhammad himself told me in Makkah: 'I will kill you'. Only my heart understands the severity of this 'prick'. By Allah! If this prick were to be distributed amongst the inhabitants of Hejaz, just this one prick would be sufficient for their destruction."

Ubayy continued bellowing like this until he reached a place called Sarif where he died.

Hadhrat Ali ﺭﺿﻲﺍﻟﻠﻪﻋﻨﻪ bathes the wounds of Rasulullah ﺻﻠﻰﺍﻟﻠﻪﻋﻠﻴﻪﻭﺳﻠﻢ

When Rasulullah ﺻﻠﻰﺍﻟﻠﻪﻋﻠﻴﻪﻭﺳﻠﻢ reached the valley, the battle had ended. He sat down whilst Hadhrat Ali ﺭﺿﻲﺍﻟﻠﻪﻋﻨﻪ brought some water and cleaned the blood off his blessed face. He also poured some water over his head. Rasulullah ﺻﻠﻰﺍﻟﻠﻪﻋﻠﻴﻪﻭﺳﻠﻢ then performed wudhu and led the Salaah whilst seated. The Sahaabah ﺭﺿﻲﺍﻟﻠﻪﻋﻨﻬﻢ also performed their Salaah whilst seated behind Rasulullah ﺻﻠﻰﺍﻟﻠﻪﻋﻠﻴﻪﻭﺳﻠﻢ.

Mutilating the corpses of the Muslims

During the battle, the disbelievers started mutilating the bodies of the Muslims. They severed the noses and ears. They ripped open their bellies and lopped off their private parts. Even the womenfolk joined the men in this gruesome task.

Hindah, whose father was killed at the hands of Hadhrat Hamzah ﺭﺿﻲﺍﻟﻠﻪﻋﻨﻪ in the battle of Badr, mutilated the body of Hadhrat Hamzah ﺭﺿﻲﺍﻟﻠﻪﻋﻨﻪ. She cut his stomach open and hacked off a piece of his liver. She then tried to swallow it but since it refused to go down her throat, she spat it out.

Elated by this satisfying moment, she removed all her jewelry and handed it over to Wahshi.

She also made a necklace out of the severed ears and noses of the Muslims and hung it around her neck.

Abu Sufyaan's taunts and Hadhrat 'Umar's رَضِيَٱللَّهُعَنْهُ reply

When the Quraysh elected to leave the battlefield, Abu Sufyaan ascended the mountain and yelled: "Is Muhammad alive amongst you?"

Rasulullah ﷺ asked his companions to refrain from responding to his provoking taunts. Abu Sufyaan yelled out thrice but each time he was greeted with absolute silence. He then called out: "Is the son of Abu Quhaafah (Abu Bakr رَضِيَٱللَّهُعَنْهُ) alive amongst you?" Rasulullah ﷺ again asked the Sahaabah رَضِيَٱللَّهُعَنْهُم to remain silent. Repeating this question three times, he kept quiet. A little while later, he asked: "Is 'Umar bin Khattaab alive?" He repeated this thrice but this statement also failed to evoke a response. He gleefully shrieked out to his cohorts: "As for that lot, they have been killed. If they were alive they would have surely responded."

However, Hadhrat 'Umar رَضِيَٱللَّهُعَنْهُ was unable to maintain his patience any longer and he screamed:

> "By Allah! You are lying, O enemy of Allah! Allah has set aside something for you that would bring grief and anguish to you."

Thereafter, taking the name of the pagan deity, Abu Sufyaan yelled:

Mount Uhud

اُعْلُ هُبَلْ اُعْلُ هُبَلْ

"Rise, O Hubal! May your religion thrive, O Hubal"

In response, Rasulullah ﷺ asked Hadhrat 'Umar ؓ to say:

اَللّٰهُ اَعْلٰى وَاَجَلُّ

"Allah is the most exalted and elevated."

Abu Sufyaan retorted:

اِنَّ لَنَا الْعُزّٰى وَلَا عُزّٰى لَكُمْ

"We have 'Uzza (name of a deity) whilst you have no 'Uzza." (In other words you have no 'Izzah, honour.)

Rasulullah ﷺ instructed Hadhrat 'Umar ؓ to reply:

اَللّٰهُ مَوْلَانَا وَلَا مَوْلٰى لَكُمْ

"Allah is our Mawlaa (Lord, master) whilst you have no Mawlaa."

In other words, honour lies only in one's association with Allah. Association with 'Uzza has no honour but dishonour.

Abu Sufyaan said:

يَوْمٌ بِيَوْمِ بَدْرٍ وَالْحَرْبُ سِجَالٌ

"This day is in response to the day of Badr. War has its ups and downs."

Hadhrat 'Umar رَضِىَ اللهُ عَنْهُ responded:

$$\text{لَا سَوَاءَ قَتْلَانَا فِي الْجَنَّةِ وَقَتْلَاكُمْ فِي النَّارِ}$$

"We can never be the same because our casualties are in Jannah whilst your victims are in Jahannam."

Since Abu Sufyaan's statement 'war has its ups and downs' was true, this statement was not responded to. Allah Ta'ala's declaration in the Qur-aan 'those are the days we rotate around people' confirms this fact.

Thereafter, Abu Sufyaan summoned Hadhrat 'Umar رَضِىَ اللهُ عَنْهُ saying: "O 'Umar! Come towards me." Rasulullah ﷺ asked Hadhrat 'Umar رَضِىَ اللهُ عَنْهُ to go and see what he wants. When Hadhrat 'Umar رَضِىَ اللهُ عَنْهُ drew closer to him, Abu Sufyaan asked:

"I beg you to pledge in the name of Allah, O 'Umar! Did we manage to kill Muhammad?"

Hadhrat 'Umar رَضِىَ اللهُ عَنْهُ replied:

"By Allah! Certainly not! He is alive and listening to you as we speak."

Abu Sufyaan commented:

"According to me, you are more truthful than Ibn Qami-ah (the celebrated wrestler of the Quraysh who was killed by a mountain goat, as explained earlier) and you are more pious than him"

Abu Sufyaan also added:

"A number of your victims were subjected to physical mutilation by our people. By Allah I swear that I am not delighted with this. I did not prevent this nor did I decree it."

As he was heading off, Abu Sufyaan cried out:

مَوْعِدُكُمْ بَدْرٌ لِلْعَامِ الْقَابِلِ

"Our meeting place is Badr in the forthcoming year."

To this Rasulullah ﷺ asked a Sahaabi to reply:

نَعَمْ هُوَ بَيْنَنَا وَ بَيْنَكَ مَوْعِدٌ اِنْشَاءَ الله

"Yes, this is a pledge between you and us, Insha Allah."

On the departure of the disbelievers from the battlefield, the womenfolk of the Muslims left Madinah to ascertain the conditions of the Muslims. Hadhrat Faatimah رضى الله عنها noticed blood running down the blessed face of Rasulullah ﷺ. Hadhrat Ali رضى الله عنه fetched some water in his shield and Hadhrat Faatimah رضى الله عنها bathed his wound. However the more she cleansed the wound, the more the blood trickled out. They then burnt a piece of a grass-mat and filled its ash into the wound. This helped in stopping the blood.

Martyrdom of S'ad bin Rab'i رضى الله عنه

Following the departure of the Quraysh, Rasulullah ﷺ instructed Zaid bin Saabit رضى الله عنه to search for the whereabouts of S'ad bin Rab'i رضى الله عنه. He instructed him thus:

"If you manage locating him, pass on my Salaam to him and inform him that the Prophet of Allah asks: 'What condition do you find yourself in now'?"

Hadhrat Zaid bin Saabit ؓ narrates: "I went out in search of him and located him whilst he still had some life left in him. He had sustained seventy sword and arrow wounds to his body. When I delivered Rasulullah's ﷺ message to him, S'ad ؓ replied:

"Salaam upon Rasulullah ﷺ and Salaam upon you as well. Inform Rasulullah ﷺ that at this moment I am able to perceive the fragrance of Jannah and inform my people, the Ansaar, that if Rasulullah ﷺ is inconvenienced in any way and they have one eye left (i.e. even if there is just one person left amongst them), none of their excuses will be accepted in the court of Allah."

Saying this, he breathed his last and bade farewell to this world.
According to another narration, S'ad bin Rab'i ؓ addressed Zaid bin Saabit ؓ thus:

"Inform Rasulullah ﷺ that at this time I am about to pass on. After conveying my Salaam to him, inform him that S'ad says: 'May Allah reward you with the best of rewards on our behalf and on behalf of the entire Ummah'."

Zaid ؓ says: "I returned to Rasulullah ﷺ and notified him of S'ad's message. He commented:

'May Allah shower His mercy upon him. In life and in death, he was loyal and he wished well for Allah and His Rasool.'"

The search for the body of Hadhrat Hamzah رَضِىَ اللّٰهُ عَنْهُ

Rasulullah ﷺ went out in search of his uncle, Hadhrat Hamzah رَضِىَ اللّٰهُ عَنْهُ. He found his mutilated body in the depth of the valley. His nose and ears were lopped off. His stomach and chest were ripped apart. On catching sight of this distressing and agonising scene, Rasulullah ﷺ was spontaneously moved to tears. He mournfully commented: "May Allah shower you with His mercy. As far as I am aware, you were exceedingly charitable and you maintained favourable family ties. If it was not for the anguish and heartache of Safiyyah[1], I would have left you like this for the vultures and beasts. They would have devoured you and on the day of judgement you would have been resurrected from their bellies."

Also standing at the same spot, Rasulullah ﷺ vowed: "By Allah I swear! If Allah grants me victory over the disbelievers, I would mutilate seventy of them in retaliation for what they have done to you."

Rasulullah ﷺ barely moved from this spot when the following verses were revealed:

$$\text{وَإِنْ عَاقَبْتُمْ فَعَاقِبُوْا بِمِثْلِ مَا عُوْقِبْتُمْ بِهٖ ۖ وَلَئِنْ صَبَرْتُمْ لَهُوَ خَيْرٌ لِّلصّٰبِرِيْنَ ۝ وَاصْبِرْ وَمَا صَبْرُكَ اِلَّا بِاللّٰهِ وَلَا تَحْزَنْ عَلَيْهِمْ وَلَا تَكُ فِيْ ضَيْقٍ مِّمَّا يَمْكُرُوْنَ ۝ اِنَّ اللّٰهَ مَعَ الَّذِيْنَ اتَّقَوْا وَّالَّذِيْنَ هُمْ مُّحْسِنُوْنَ ۝}$$

"And if you retaliate then retaliate to the extent of the adversity you were afflicted with. And if you exercise patience, it is best for the patient ones.

---

[1] Hadhrat Safiyyah رَضِىَ اللّٰهُ عَنْهَا was the sister of Hadhrat Hamzah رَضِىَ اللّٰهُ عَنْهُ

And exercise patience, your patience is only with the divine guidance of Allah, do not be grieved over them (disbelievers) and do not be distressed by what they plot. Verily, Allah is with those who have Taqwa (Allah-consciousness) and with those who do well."

Rasulullah ﷺ then exercised patience, paid kaffaarah (expiation) for breaking his oath and abandoned this idea (of retaliation).

Hadhrat Jaabir رضي الله عنه narrates that when Rasulullah ﷺ glimpsed at the body of Hadhrat Hamzah رضي الله عنه, he burst out crying and in a sobbing voice he declared:

سَيِّدُ الشُّهَدَاءِ عِنْدَ اللهِ يَوْمَ الْقِيَامَةِ حَمْزَةُ

"On the day of Qiyaamah, Hamzah would be the leader of all the martyrs in the sight of Allah."

This is why he was distinguished with the title of Sayyidus-Shuhadaa.

Martyrdom of Usayrim رضي الله عنه

'Amr bin Saabit who was commonly known by his title Usayrim always remained aloof from Islam. He was initially reluctant to embrace Islam. On the day of Uhud, Islam penetrated his heart and clutching a sword in his hand, he strode onto the battlefield and valiantly fought the disbelievers until he fell down wounded. When the people discovered that it was Usayrim, they were stunned and asked: "O 'Amr! What prompted you of all people to engage in this battle? Were you prompted by an earnest desire for Islam or was it due to your loyalty to your nationality and your patriotism?"

Usayrim replied:

"In fact my participation in this battle was prompted solely by my earnest desire for Islam. So I embraced Islam and put my faith in Allah and His Rasool and clutching a sword I fought on the side of Rasulullah ﷺ until I was afflicted with these wounds."

He barely finished uttering these words when he left this world.

اِنَّهُ لَمِنْ اَهْلِ الْجَنَّةِ

"Surely he is amongst the inhabitants of Jannah."

Hadhrat Abu Hurayrah ؓ would often ask: "Tell me, who was admitted into Jannah without performing a single Salaah?" It was none other than this Sahaabi ؓ.

Since some horrific stories about the war had reached Madinah, the men, women, children and the elderly were eager to see Rasulullah ﷺ safe and sound, more than their own relatives.

Hadhrat S'ad bin Abi Waqqaas ؓ narrates: "On his return from this battle, Rasulullah ﷺ passed by an Ansaari woman who lost her husband, brother and father in this battle. When she was informed of the martyrdom of her husband, brother and father, she asked: 'No, tell me how is Rasulullah ﷺ?' The people replied: 'Alhamdulillah! He is well.' The lady replied: 'Show me his blessed face. I will be at ease once I set eyes on him.' When the people pointed out Rasulullah ﷺ to her, she exclaimed: 'Every calamity after you is trivial and insignificant.'"

Shrouding and Burial of the Martyrs

In this battle, seventy Sahaabah رَضِيَاللَّهُعَنْهُم were martyred, most of them were from the Ansaar. They were so destitute that they did not even possess sufficient cloth to shroud their dead. When Mus'ab bin 'Umair رَضِيَاللَّهُعَنْهُ was martyred, the sheet for his burial shroud was so short that when his head was covered, his feet would be exposed and when his feet were covered his face would be exposed. Eventually, Rasulullah صَلَّىاللَّهُعَلَيْهِوَسَلَّم advised them to cover his head with the sheet and his feet with izkhir leaves.

A similar incident is recorded about Sayyidush-Shuhadaa Hadhrat Hamzah رَضِيَاللَّهُعَنْهُ.

Some of the martyrs could not afford even a single sheet of cloth. Some of them were shrouded in pairs with a single sheet of cloth between the two of them, and then in sets of twos and threes, they were buried in a single grave. At the time of burial, Rasulullah صَلَّىاللَّهُعَلَيْهِوَسَلَّم would ask: "Who knows more of the Qur-aan from amongst them?" He would then place whoever was pointed out to him towards the front of the grave facing the Qiblah. The others would then be placed behind him. Rasulullah صَلَّىاللَّهُعَلَيْهِوَسَلَّم would then remark:

$$\text{اَنَا شَهِيْدٌ عَلَى هٰؤُلَاءِ يَوْمَ الْقِيَامَةِ}$$

"I will bear witness in their favour on the day of Qiyaamah."

Rasulullah صَلَّىاللَّهُعَلَيْهِوَسَلَّم also instructed them to bury these martyrs without ghusl in their same blood-spattered clothing. Some of the Sahaabah رَضِيَاللَّهُعَنْهُم expressed a desire to take the bodies of their loved ones back to

Madinah for burial but Rasulullah ﷺ turned them down and bade them to bury their dead where they were martyred.

Visiting the battlefield of Uhud should bring back the memories of the great sacrifices made by the Sahaabah *(radiyallahu anhum)* and how they gave their lives for Islam. We also learn from this battle the importance of holding firmly to the instructions of Rasulullah ﷺ in every facet of our lives.

CHAPTER Ten

The Battle of Khandaq (Trench)

After spending some time at the Battlefield of Uhud, our driver took us to a place approximately 700 meters away from Masjidun Nabawi called Sab'ah Masaajid. (seven Masjids). This is the place where the Battle of Khandaq had taken place. These seven masaajid were built in the hollow of Mount Sala and each of these Masaajid mark the spots where Nabi ﷺ made dua to Allah Ta'ala for victory against the Quraish and its allies.

Standing on the battle ground of Khandaq refreshes the memories of the great sacrifices and the bravery of Nabi ﷺ and His noble Sahaabah *(radiyallahu anhum)*. It was here that Hadhrat Ali رضي الله عنه slayed the warrior 'Amr ibn Abdu Wud who was known to be the bravest soldier of the Kuffaar. It was here that Nabi ﷺ tied two stones to his mubaarak stomach out of extreme hunger. Hadhrat Sa'd bin Muaaz رضي الله عنه, the leader of the Aus tribe, had given his life in this battle. Such was his passing away that the Arsh of Allah Ta'ala shook at his demise. Standing on the top of the mountain at the entrance of Masjid-e-Fatah, reminds the visitor to renew his pledge with Allah Ta'ala to sacrifice everything for Allah Ta'ala and His Rasul ﷺ.

Hadhrat Moulana Siddeeq Ahmad Bandwi Saahib *(rahmatullahi alayh)* has mentioned that upto this day if a visitor sincerely makes dua to Allah Ta'ala at Masjid-e-Fatah, his duas will be answered. We stopped for a short while at this masjid, performed two rakaats Tahiyyatul Masjid and then spent some time making dua to Allah Ta'ala.

Below is a vivid description of this great battle explained in the words of the great Muhaddith, Hadhrat Moulana Idrees Kandhlawi *(rahmatullahi alayh)*.

The Battle

The Battle of Khandaq took place in the year 5 A.H. On their return from the Battle of Uhud, Abu Sufyaan made a threatening statement to the Muslims warning them that he would fight them the following year. Saying this he returned to Makkah Mukarramah. In the following year, as the time to carry out his threat drew closer, he left Makkah Mukarramah but returned en route citing reasons of drought and the inappropriateness of war. A year later, he attempted to launch an attack against Madinah Munawwarah with a force of 10 000 men. This expedition is referred to as the expedition of Khandaq or the expedition of Ahzaab.

The main reason for this expedition was the banishing of the Banu Nazeer. Huyayy bin Akhtab, the leader of the Banu Nazeer, went to Makkah Mukarramah and incited the Quraysh to take up arms against Rasulullah ﷺ. Meanwhile Kinaanah ibn Rab'i approached the

Banu Ghitfaan tribe and persuaded them to go into battle against Rasulullah ﷺ. Kinaanah tempted them to agree by offering them half the produce of the palm trees of Khaybar annually. On hearing this pledge, 'Uyaynah bin Hisn Fazaari (their chief) swiftly agreed. The Quraysh, on the other hand, were eager to fight from the very outset (so there was no need to entice them any further).

This is how Abu Sufyaan, with a force of 10 000 strong, set out towards Madinah Munawwarah to annihilate the Muslims once and for all.

When Rasulullah ﷺ heard of their departure from Makkah Mukarramah, he consulted the Sahaabah ﵁. Hadhrat Salmaan Faarsi ﵁ proposed the digging of trenches around the city. He explained that it would be somewhat difficult to fight them on the open field. Fighting them from the protection of the trenches would be more appropriate. This proposal appealed to all the Sahaabah ﵁.

Rasulullah ﷺ himself set its boundaries, drew lines and assigned ten people per ten yards (9.1 meters) for the digging of the trenches.

The trenches were dug so deep that they encountered the moisture of the soil. The trenches were completed in six days.

Rasulullah ﷺ also physically joined the Sahaabah ﵁ in digging the trenches. He struck the very first pick to the ground with his blessed hands and the following words were on his blessed tongue:

$$\text{بِسْمِ اللهِ وَبِهِ بَدِيْنَا وَلَوْ عَبَدْنَا غَيْرَهُ شَقِيْنَا}$$

"Bismillah, we commence in the name of Allah. If we worshipped anyone other than Him, we would surely be doomed to an ill fate.

$$\text{حَبَّذَا رَبًّا وَحَبَّذَا دِيْنًا}$$

Oh, what a wonderful Rabb He is and what a magnificent religion we have!"

It was during the midst of winter. Icy cold winds were blowing and they were starving for a few days but the devoted Muhaajireen and Ansaar were enthusiastically engaged in digging the trenches. Whilst occupied in shifting mounds of sand, they would chant the following words:

$$\text{نَحْنُ الَّذِيْنَ بَايَعُوْا مُحَمَّدَا عَلَى الْجِهَادِ مَا بَقِيْنَا اَبَدَا}$$

"We are those who pledged on the hands of Muhammad ﷺ (and we have sold our lives to Allah for Rasulullah ﷺ) that we would continue fighting in Jihaad as long as we have life within us."

In response to these words, Rasulullah ﷺ would call out:

$$\text{اَللّٰهُمَّ لَا عَيْشَ اِلَّا عَيْشُ الْاٰخِرَةِ فَاغْفِرْ لِلْاَنْصَارِ وَالْمُهَاجِرَةِ}$$

"O Allah! There is really no life but the life of the hereafter. So forgive the Ansaar and the Muhaajireen."

Hadhrat Baraa bin 'Aazib رضي الله عنه narrates: "On the day of the trench, Rasulullah ﷺ himself was engaged in carrying the sand of the trenches to such an extent that his blessed stomach turned grimy with dust. Whilst carrying the sand, he would call out the following words:

$$\text{وَاللهِ لَوْ لَا اللهُ مَا اهْتَدَيْنَا وَلَا تَصَدَّقْنَا وَلَا صَلَّيْنَا}$$

By Allah! If it was not for the divine guidance of Allah, we would not have been guided, neither would we have performed our Salaah nor disbursed charity.

$$\text{فَاَنْزِلَنْ سَكِيْنَةً عَلَيْنَا} \quad \text{وَثَبِّتِ الْاَقْدَامَ اِنْ لَاقَيْنَا}$$

O Allah! Shower us with tranquility and keep us steadfast when we are confronted by the enemy.

$$\text{اِنَّ الْاُلٰى قَدْ بَغَوْا عَلَيْنَا} \quad \text{اِذَا اَرَادُوْا فِتْنَةً اَبَيْنَا اَبَيْنَا اَبَيْنَا...}$$

They have been vindictive to us. If they wish to turn us to wrong, we will flatly refuse." (At the end of this stanza are the words Abaynaa, Abaynaa (we will refuse, we will refuse).

Whilst Rasulullah ﷺ was singing these stanzas, as he came to the end, he would repeatedly recite in a loud tone: "Abaynaa Abaynaa Abaynaa..."

Confronted by a huge boulder

Hadhrat Jaabir ؓ narrates: "Whilst digging the trenches, we were confronted by a huge boulder. When we raised this issue with Rasulullah ﷺ, he replied: 'Wait, I will go down into the trench myself.' Due to severe hunger, Rasulullah ﷺ had tied a stone to his abdomen. We too had not eaten anything for three days. Rasulullah ﷺ gripped the pickaxe with his blessed hands and landed three blows to the boulder turning it to a mound of sand."

When Rasulullah ﷺ landed the first blow with the pickaxe, a third of the boulder shattered and he remarked: "Allahu Akbar! I have been awarded the keys of the kingdom of Syria. By Allah! At this moment, I can see the red palaces of Syria." When Rasulullah ﷺ struck the boulder a second time, another third broke off and he remarked: "Allahu Akbar! I have been awarded the keys to Persia. By Allah! At this moment I can perceive with my very eyes the white palace of Madaain." When Rasulullah ﷺ struck the boulder a third time, the rest of it shattered and he said: "Allahu Akbar! I have been awarded the keys to Yemen. By Allah, from where I am standing, I can clearly see the doors of Sanaa."

According to another narration, when Rasulullah ﷺ struck the boulder the first time, a bolt of lightning flashed in the sky illuminating the palaces of Syria. To this Rasulullah ﷺ remarked: "Allahu Akbar!" This Takbeer was then also echoed by the Sahaabah رضي الله عنهم. Thereafter, Rasulullah ﷺ said: "Jibraa'eel Ameen just informed me that my Ummah is destined to conquer all those cities."

The armies of the Quraish arrive in Madinah Munawwarah

The Muslims barely completed the digging of the trenches when the ten-thousand-strong well-equipped army of the Quraysh landed on the outskirts of Madinah Munawwarah. They set up base near Mount Uhud. With a force of 3000 Sahaabah رضي الله عنهم, Rasulullah ﷺ set out to confront them and set up camp near Mount Sala. The trenches were separating both the armies. Rasulullah ﷺ directed all women and children to be secured in one of the fortresses.

The Jews break their treaty

Until that moment, the Banu Qurayzah were still neutral. However, the leader of the Banu Nazeer, Huyayy bin Akhtab tried every possible means to win them over as allies against the Muslims. Huyayy bin Akhtab, the leader of the Banu Nazeer tribe, personally went to K'ab bin Asad, the leader of the Banu Qurayzah, who had already signed a peace treaty with Rasulullah ﷺ. The moment K'ab caught sight of Huyayy coming, he slammed the fortress door shut. Huyayy shouted: "Open the door. (I wish to speak to you)."

K'ab responded: "Shame on you, O Huyayy! You are certainly an ill-fated man. I have already entered into a pact with Muhammad and I will definitely not violate this agreement because I have not witnessed anything from him but truthfulness, honesty and execution of his promises."

Huyayy, not wanting to be put down any further, pleaded: "Allow me to present before you something that would guarantee you eternal honour. I have brought the forces of Quraysh and Ghitfaan right up to your doorstep. All of us have pledged never to budge an inch until Muhammad and his companions are utterly annihilated."

K'ab replied: "By Allah! You always bring humiliation and shame in your wake. I will never ever breach the treaty with Muhammad. I haven't witnessed anything from him but truthfulness, honesty and fulfillment of his promises."

However, Huyayy was not a person to be easily swayed. He persisted in his efforts to influence K'ab until K'ab ultimately agreed to break his commitment with Rasulullah ﷺ.

When Rasulullah ﷺ was informed of their treachery, he sent S'ad bin Mu'aaz ؓ, S'ad bin 'Ubaadah ؓ and Abdullah bin

Rawaahah ؓ to make further investigations. He also advised them: "If this news proves to be correct, return and inform me in such ambiguous terms that the ordinary person would not be able to grasp its meaning and if this news proves to be incorrect, there is no problem in revealing it publicly."

When this group went to K'ab bin Asad and reminded him about their mutual agreement, he retorted: "What agreement? What pact? And who is Muhammad? I do not ever remember making a pact with him."

When this group returned to Rasulullah ﷺ, they merely said: "Adal and Qaarah." In other words, just as the tribes of 'Adal and Qaarah acted treacherously with Ashaab-e-Raj'i (Hadhrat Khubaib ؓ and his companions), similarly, these Jews are also guilty of treachery.

Rasulullah ﷺ was immensely disheartened over their betrayal and treachery. Now the Muslims were surrounded by the disbelievers from all sides. The outside enemies, resembling a swarm of locusts, were camped right before them whilst the enemies from within the siege, (the Banu Qurayzah), also linked up with them. In short, the Muslims were facing overwhelming odds and to top this, the nights were bitterly cold and they were starving for a number of days.

Allah Ta'ala describes this scenario in Surah Ahzaab in the following words:

$$اِذْ جَآءُوْ كُمْ مِّنْ فَوْقِكُمْ وَ مِنْ اَسْفَلَ مِنْكُمْ وَ اِذْ زَاغَتِ الْاَبْصَارُ وَ بَلَغَتِ الْقُلُوْبُ الْحَنَاجِرَ وَ تَظُنُّوْنَ بِاللهِ الظُّنُوْنَا ۝ هُنَالِكَ ابْتُلِيَ الْمُؤْمِنُوْنَ وَ زُلْزِلُوْا زِلْزَالًا شَدِيْدًا ۝$$

"Remember when the enemy came upon you from above and from beneath you, and when the eyes were dazzled (with fright) and the hearts

reached the throats (in horror) and you started harbouring suspicions about Allah. There, the believers were tested and were powerfully shaken." [Surah Ahzaab verses 10-11]

The hypocrites turn away from the Battle

This was a trial for the Muslims. Sincerity and hypocrisy were being screened on the 'scales of trials'. These scales separated the genuine from the fake. Alarmed by the current events, the hypocrites launched into all forms of lame excuses. Some of them said: "O Rasulullah! Due to the low walls, our houses are not safe. The safety of our wives and children is crucial. So we appeal to you to allow us to leave."

The Qur-aan Shareef describes this thus:

$$\text{يَقُولُونَ اِنَّ بُيُوتَنَا عَوْرَةٌ ۛ وَمَا هِىَ بِعَوْرَةٍ ۛ اِنْ يُرِيدُونَ اِلَّا فِرَارًا}$$

"They (the hypocrites) say: 'Our homes lie exposed (to the enemy).' But they are not exposed. They merely wish to flee. (This is why they are offering lame excuses.)" [Surah Ahzaab. Verse 13]

Allah Ta'ala describes the Muslims, whose hearts were infused with sincerity and true faith, thus:

$$\text{وَلَمَّا رَاَ الْمُؤْمِنُونَ الْاَحْزَابَ ۙ قَالُوا هٰذَا مَا وَعَدَنَا اللّٰهُ وَ رَسُولُهٗ وَ صَدَقَ اللّٰهُ وَ رَسُولُهٗ ۙ وَمَا زَادَهُمْ اِلَّا اِيْمَانًا وَّ تَسْلِيْمًا}$$

"When the believers caught sight of the Allies (Ahzaab), they said: 'This is what Allah and His Messenger had promised us and Allah and His

Battle of Khandaq (Trench)

Messenger had spoken the truth'. And this only enhanced their faith and submission." [Surah Ahzaab verse 22]

Nonetheless, the Jews as well as the hypocrites acted treacherously and deceptively on this expedition. The Muslims were thus wedged in on all sides by an enemy frm the outside and an enemy from within. Due to the frustrating difficulties of the siege, Rasulullah ﷺ thought that perhaps the Muslims, driven by natural human nature, would be thrown into a cauldron of panic and anxiety. This is why Rasulullah ﷺ proposed that a peace treaty be fostered with 'Uyaynah bin Hisn and Haaris bin 'Awf (both leaders of the Ghitfaan tribes) by offering them a third of the produce of the palm orchards of Madinah Munawwarah. This proposal, Rasulullah ﷺ deduced, would drive them away from supporting Abu Sufyaan and also somewhat relieve the current siege. Subsequently, Rasulullah ﷺ expressed this idea before S'ad bin Mu'aaz رضي الله عنه and S'ad bin 'Ubaadah رضي الله عنه. They replied: "O Rasulullah (ﷺ!) Did Allah Ta'ala command you to do this? If yes, it would only be our pleasure to execute this divine commandment or are you proposing this merely out of affection and compassion for us?" Rasulullah ﷺ replied: "This is not a divine commandment of Allah. This is merely a suggestion on my part with your best interests at heart. All the Arabs have united their forces against you and they are 'raining down arrows onto you from a single bow'. With the strategy I have in mind, I wish to undermine their united stance and chip away at their cohesive strength."

Hadhrat S'ad bin Mu'aaz رضي الله عنه submitted: "O Rasulullah ﷺ! When all of us were disbelievers, we worshipped idols. We had no idea whatsoever about Allah Ta'ala. Even at that time none of them had the courage to take a single bunch of dates from us except as a guest or by purchasing it from us. And now when Allah Ta'ala has blessed us with this incomparable gift of Hidaayat (divine guidance) and honoured us with Islam, must we surrender our wealth to them? This is impossible! By Allah! We have no need to relinquish our wealth to these people. By Allah! We will present them with nothing but the sword. They may do as they deem fit."

Hadhrat S'ad bin Mu'aaz رضى الله عنه then took hold of Rasulullah's ﷺ blessed hand and rubbed out the entire text of the proposed peace agreement that was written down in this respect.

Two weeks passed like this without any actual combat. During these two weeks, both sides merely engaged in lobbing arrows at one another. At length, a few mounted warriors of the Quraysh; 'Amr bin 'Abduwudd, 'Ikramah bin Abi Jahal, Hubairah bin Abi Wahab, Diraar bin Khattaab and Nawfal bin Abdullah, stepped out to engage the Muslims. When they reached the trenches, they remarked: "By Allah! We've never had such deceptive tactics amongst the Arabs before this."

Quraishi warriors cross over the trench

One section of the trench was a bit narrow. They managed to breach this weak spot, scaled over and challengingly roused the Muslims to step out for hand-to-hand combat. Amr bin 'Abduwudd, who had dropped down wounded in the Battle of Badr, was encased in a full-body armour covering him from head to toe. In a menacing tone, he hailed: "Is there anyone who dares to take me on?" In response to this challenge, the lion of Allah, Hadhrat Ali رضى الله عنه stepped forth and said: "O 'Amr! I call you unto Allah and His Rasul ﷺ. I invite you towards Islam." 'Amr disdainfully replied: "I have no need for such things." Hadhrat Ali رضى الله عنه said: "Okay, I now invite you to fight with me." 'Amr replied: "You are still a youngster. Send me someone elder than you. I hate killing someone as young as you." Hadhrat Ali رَضِيَ اللَّهُ عَنْهُ replied: "But I would love to kill you." This drove him into a blind rage. He dismounted from his horse and marched up to Hadhrat Ali رَضِيَ اللَّهُ عَنْهُ. At once, he attacked Hadhrat Ali رَضِيَ اللَّهُ عَنْهُ with his sword. He managed to deflect the strike with his shield but was slightly wounded on his forehead. Hadhrat Ali رَضِيَ اللَّهُ عَنْهُ then launched an attack on him and finished him off for good.

Hadhrat Ali رَضِيَ اللَّهُ عَنْهُ yelled out the Takbeer of Allahu Akbar! This was a sign to the Muslims of his triumph over his enemy.

Nawfal bin Abdullah advanced with the sole intention of assassinating Rasulullah صَلَّى اللَّهُ عَلَيْهِ وَسَلَّمَ. He was mounted on a horse. He attempted to leap across the trench but he fell into it and broke his neck. The disbelievers tendered 10 000 Dirhams to Rasulullah صَلَّى اللَّهُ عَلَيْهِ وَسَلَّمَ in exchange of Nawfal's body but Rasulullah صَلَّى اللَّهُ عَلَيْهِ وَسَلَّمَ responded: "He was filthy and the diyat (blood money) offered is also filthy. Allah's curse is upon him and his blood money. We have absolutely no need for his 10 000 nor for his body for that matter." Rasulullah صَلَّى اللَّهُ عَلَيْهِ وَسَلَّمَ then relinquished his body without any form of exchange.

Sa'd bin Muaaz's رَضِيَ اللَّهُ عَنْهُ spirit for martyrdom

S'ad bin Mu'aaz رَضِيَ اللَّهُ عَنْهُ was struck on his jugular by an arrow. He made the following dua:

O Allah! If this battle with the Quraysh is bound to last (for some time) then make me last also accordingly because I have no yearning greater than fighting the people who subjected Your Messenger to such hardship, falsified him and evicted him from the safe Haram. O Allah! If this is the end of the war, make this injury a source of my martyrdom and do not take my life away until I am able to cool my eyes with the humiliation of the Banu Qurayzah."

This was one of the fiercest days of the battle. Most of the day passed in encountering and launching arrows and rocks. In this turbulence, Rasulullah ﷺ missed four Salaah.

Bravery of Hadhrat Safiyyah رضى الله عنها

Rasulullah ﷺ had secured the women and children in one of the forts. The fort was in close proximity to the locality of one of the Jewish tribes. Hadhrat Safiyyah رضى الله عنها, Rasulullah's ﷺ father's sister was also confined to the fort. Hadhrat Hassaan رضى الله عنه was appointed to keep guard over the fort. Hadhrat Safiyyah رضى الله عنها caught sight of a Jew wandering about the fort. She feared that he may be a spy or he may be engaged in some wicked activity. She addressed Hadhrat Hassaan رضى الله عنه: "Go out and kill him. He should not divulge any information about us to the enemy." He replied: "Don't you know? I am not appointed for that purpose and I am incapable of doing such a thing." Hadhrat Safiyyah رضى الله عنها then decided to take matters into her own hands; she got hold of a tent peg and struck the Jew with such force that his head cracked open. She told Hassaan رضى الله عنه: "He is a man and I am a woman. So I cannot touch him. Go and take off his weapons." Hadhrat Hassaan رضى الله عنه replied: "I have no need for his weapons and goods."

War strategy

During the course of the siege, one of the chieftains of the Ghitfaan tribe, Nu'aim bin Mas'ood Ashja'i appeared in the presence of Rasulullah ﷺ and submitted: "O Rasulullah! I have embraced Islam and I believe in you. My people are ignorant about my accepting Islam. Subject to your approval, I wish to embark on a strategy that would eliminate this blockade." Rasulullah ﷺ replied: "Sure. You are a man of great experience. If such a manoeuvre is possible, go for it because after all 'war is deception'."

Subsequently, Nu'aim ؓ initiated such a deceptive strategy in motion which destroyed the alliance between the Banu Qurayzah and the Quraysh. This forced the Banu Qurayzah to withdraw all forms of support they offered to the Quraysh.

Following the deaths of 'Amr bin Abduwudd and Nawfal, the remaining Qurayshi warriors (who had managed to breach the trench) made a hasty retreat in defeat.

Hadhrat Abu Sa'eed Khudri ؓ narrates: "Citing the strain and harshness of this siege, we pleaded with Rasulullah ﷺ to make dua for us. Rasulullah ﷺ replied: "Make the following dua:

$$\text{اَللّٰهُمَّ اسْتُرْ عَوْرَاتِنَا وَاٰمِنْ رَوْعَاتِنَا}$$

"O Allah! Conceal our shortcomings and eliminate the source of our fear."

Rasulullah ﷺ also made the following dua:

$$\text{اَللّٰهُمَّ مُنْزِلَ الْكِتَابِ وَمُجْرِيَ السَّحَابِ وَهَازِمَ الْاَحْزَابِ اِهْزِمْهُمْ وَانْصُرْنَا عَلَيْهِمْ}$$

"O Allah! The revealer of the divine book, the driver of the clouds, the conqueror of the allies! Defeat them and shower us with Your divine assistance."

Unseen help of Allah Ta'ala

Allah Ta'ala accepted this dua of Rasulullah ﷺ. He subjected the Quraysh and Ghitfaan to such a violent wind that uprooted their tents. The tent-ropes snapped. Cauldrons and other utensils overturned. A steady stream of sand and rough particles blowing into the eyes, threw the entire army of the disbelievers into utter confusion and absolute disorder. In this regard Allah Ta'ala revealed the following verse:

$$\text{يَاأَيُّهَا الَّذِيْنَ اٰمَنُوا اذْكُرُوا نِعْمَةَ اللّٰهِ عَلَيْكُمْ اِذْ جَآءَتْكُمْ جُنُوْدٌ فَاَرْسَلْنَا عَلَيْهِمْ رِيْحًا وَّ جُنُوْدًا لَّمْ تَرَوْهَا ۚ وَ كَانَ اللّٰهُ بِمَا تَعْمَلُوْنَ بَصِيْرًا}$$

"O you who believe! Remember the favour of Allah upon you when a number of armies came to you. So We despatched upon them (the disbelievers) a wind and such forces, which you were unable to perceive (i.e. angels). And Allah is watchful over your actions." [Surah Ahzaab verse 9]

In this verse, the phrase 'forces which you were unable to perceive' refers to the angels who infused terror and anxiety into the hearts of the disbelievers whilst fortifying the hearts of the Muslims. In this manner, a ten-thousand-strong force of the disbelievers fled in abject disarray. As Allah Ta'ala says:

$$\text{وَ رَدَّ اللّٰهُ الَّذِيْنَ كَفَرُوْا بِغَيْظِهِمْ لَمْ يَنَالُوْا خَيْرًا ۚ وَ كَفَى اللّٰهُ الْمُؤْمِنِيْنَ الْقِتَالَ ۚ وَ كَانَ اللّٰهُ قَوِيًّا عَزِيْزًا}$$

"Despite the rage of the disbelievers, Allah drove them back. They gained no good (booty). Allah sufficed for the believers in the fighting (by sending a wind and angels against the disbelievers). And Allah is strong and mighty." [Surah Ahzaab verse 25]

Hadhrat Huzayfah رضى الله عنه spies on the enemy

Hadhrat Huzayfah bin Yamaan رضى الله عنه narrates: "Rasulullah ﷺ instructed me to gather some information about the Quraysh. I submitted: "I fear being captured by the enemy." Rasulullah ﷺ replied: "Never! You will never be captured." Rasulullah ﷺ then made the following dua for me:

"O Allah! Protect him from his front, from behind him, from his right, from his left, from above and from beneath him."

Due to this dua of Rasulullah ﷺ, all my anxieties faded away and with a sense of elation I set off. As I was leaving, Rasulullah ﷺ cautioned: "Huzayfah! Avoid doing anything unwarranted."

When I crept into their camp, the wind was blowing so fiercely that nothing was motionless and the night was so dark that nothing was visible. As I drew closer to them, I heard Abu Sufyaan muttering: "O people of the Quraysh! This is not a place for us to remain any longer. Our animals have perished, Banu Qurayzah have abandoned us and this wind has hurled us all into a state of utter confusion. Moving about or even sitting here is almost unbearable. It is best for us to return without delay." Saying this, Abu Sufyaan mounted his camel.

Hadhrat Huzayfah رضى الله عنه narrates: "At that instant I thought of shooting an arrow at him but the words of Rasulullah ﷺ came to mind that, 'Huzayfah! Avoid doing anything unwarranted'. I then returned to our base."

As the Quraysh started retreating, Rasulullah ﷺ remarked:

> "Now we will attack them and they will not attack us. We will now advance and launch an offensive attack against them."

In other words, the forces of kufr have become so weak that they lack the courage to take offensive action against Islam, with Islam merely taking a defensive stance. On the contrary, now Islam has turned into such a powerful force that it will launch offensive strikes against the forces of kufr instead of just taking defensive measures against them.

Early the next morning, Rasulullah ﷺ made preparations to return to Madinah Munawwarah and the following words were on his blessed tongue:

لَا اِلٰهَ اِلَّا اللهُ وَحْدَهُ لَا شَرِيْكَ لَهُ لَهُ الْمُلْكُ وَلَهُ الْحَمْدُ وَهُوَ عَلٰى كُلِّ شَيْءٍ قَدِيْرٌ اٰئِبُوْنَ تَائِبُوْنَ عَابِدُوْنَ سَاجِدُوْنَ لِرَبِّنَا حَامِدُوْنَ صَدَقَ اللهُ وَعْدَهُ وَ نَصَرَ عَبْدَهُ وَهَزَمَ الْاَحْزَابَ وَحْدَهُ

> "There is none worthy of worship but Allah. He has no partner. To Him belongs all supremacy and praise and He has absolute control over everything. We have returned, we are repentant, we are prostrate before our Rabb and we praise Him Alone. Allah has fulfilled His promise, assisted His servant and defeated the allies all Alone."

The siege lasted for fifteen days.

Battle of Khandaq (Trench)

In this expedition, the disbelievers lost three men;

1. Nawfal bin Abdullah,
2. 'Amr bin Abduwudd and
3. Maniyyah bin 'Ubaid

Six people died as martyrs from the Muslims. They were:

1. S'ad bin Mu'aaz رضى الله عنه
2. Anas bin Uwais رضى الله عنه
3. Abdullah bin Sahal رضى الله عنه
4. Tufail bin Nu'maan رضى الله عنه
5. Sa'labah bin 'Anamah رضى الله عنه
6. K'ab bin Zaid رضى الله عنه

The visitor to Mount Sala should spend some time visualizing the battle scene before him. The Sahaabah *(radiyallahu anhum)* sacrificed everything for Rasulullah ﷺ and his mission. May Allah Ta'ala reward them with the greatest rewards. They set such a lofty example that none will ever be able to imitate them. Let the visit to khandaq be a reminder to show our love and allegiance to Islam in an attempt to imitate the noble Sahaabah *(radiyallahu anhum)*.

CHAPTER Eleven

Leaving Madinah Munawwarah

The most difficult moment for the visitor to Madinah Munawwarah is when he has to leave this beautiful city. No Muslim wishes to leave this garden of Jannah. The poet says:

تمنا ہے کہ گلزارِ مدینہ اب وطن ہوتا   وہاں کے گلشنوں میں کوئی اپنا بھی چمن ہوتا

How I wish Madinah Munawwarah was my home, And that I had my own little garden in the gardens of Madinah.

One's heart automatically feels heavy and tears involuntarily flow from the eyes. How difficult is it to leave the surroundings of the beloved. If only we could just confirm a place for ourselves in the court of Rasulullah ﷺ.

Leaving Madinah Munawwarah

Hadhrat Shaikh Zakariyya *(rahmatullahi alayh)* advises: "Before leaving Madinah Munawwarah, perform two rakaats salaah in Masjidun Nabawi, preferably in the Riyaadhul Jannah. Then make a farewell salaam to Rasulullah ﷺ. Let the last salaam be an extraordinary salaam. Try to lengthen your final moments at the Raudha Mubaarak. Present your final salaam with a heavy heart with tears flowing from your eyes and your heart filled with sorrow as you depart from our beloved Nabi ﷺ.

Make dua to Allah Ta'ala to accept your ziyaarah. Also make dua for all your needs, as well as a safe return home and that this should not be your last presence in Madinah Shareef. Let tears flow at the time of leaving. If tears do not flow, then at least imitate those who cry. When leaving, give out charity to the poor people of Madinah Munawwarah and read the masnoon duas that are normally read when returning from somewhere. Leave now in the sunnah manner."

Aah! The city of Madinah! As you are leaving, keep your tongue busy with the recitation of Durood Shareef. Look at every particle of the city of Madinah Munawwarah with love and infatuation. Never ever allow words of disapproval to pass your lips. Think how fortunate you are that for a few days Allah Ta'ala took you out of the thorns of this world and brought you amongst the flowers of Jannah. This is that place where Allah's Deen had taken root. This is where we learnt how to live as human beings. This is where insaaniyat was taught to the Ummat. If we had not attained guidance from here, Allah protect, Allah protect, we don't know which temple or church we may have ended up in. All praise be to Allah Ta'ala who guided us to Islam and Imaan. What have we done to thank Allah Ta'ala in return for all these favours?

The lesson of Madinah Munawwarah

Madinah Munawwarah is the markaz of Islam and Deen. When leaving Madinah, take with you as much as you please from this mubaarak city and pass it on to the rest of the Ummat. Take the ajwa khajoor (dates) of this mubaarak land, take the sand of Madinah which is a cure for all illnesses, take the other *tabarrukaat* (blessings) of this place, but don't forget to take the main gift of Madinah, i.e. the gift of serving the Deen of Allah Ta'ala.

Every piece of ground in Madinah, every grain of sand in Baqee and every pebble in Mount Uhud conveys this message. These were the men who migrated from Makkah Mukarramah. What were they short of in Makkah? They had the greatest blessings in Makkah Mukarramah. The reward for one salaah equals to the reward of 100 000 salaah. The special mercies of Allah Ta'ala are descending all the time in Makkah. Malaaikah throng around the Haram Shareef. 70 000 Malaaikah are making tawaaf of the Baitullah daily. The question is what were they short of in Makkah?

The answer is, the opportunity of serving Deen openly and freely. Living and dying for Deen. Coming to Madinah Munawwarah gave them the opportunity of passing the message of Islam to the Ummat. Indeed they fulfilled this responsibility to its fullest. They sacrificed everything for Deen to spread to the four corners of the world. May Allah Ta'ala reward them with the greatest reward.

Leave Madinah Munawwarah with this frame of mind that "I will leave as an ambassador of Rasulullah ﷺ and spread the word of Allah Ta'ala to the four corners of the world."

When the Sahaabah of Nabi Muhammad ﷺ left Madinah Munawwarah, they left with this intention. Muaaz bin Jabal ؓ cried

Leaving Madinah Munawwarah

bitterly as he left Nabi ﷺ. Nabi ﷺ walked him right out of Madinah. Why would he want to leave Madinah? Why would he want to leave the noble company of Rasulullah ﷺ? It was only for the sake of serving Deen that he left Madinah Munawwarah to settle in Yemen.

O visitor of Madinah! As you leave the enlightened city, keep the following intentions within your heart;

1. I will try my best to bring every sunnat alive in my life as well as amongst all people.
2. I will try to increase my recitation of Durood Shareef daily.
3. I will try to make the mission of my life the mission for which Nabi Muhammad ﷺ had come and that is to live for Deen and die for Deen.
4. I will not hesitate to make any sacrifice at any time for the sake of Allah Ta'ala and His Rasul ﷺ.

اگرچہ غرق دریائے گناہ ہم   فتادہ خشک لب بر خاک راہم

Indeed we are sinners, drowned in the sea of our sins. Yet great is the thirst of our endeavour to follow your way

The people of Madinah Munawwarah had traversed vast lands and crossed deep oceans to bring this beautiful Deen to us. They placed it on a platter before us with love and affection and served it to us with respect and honour. All we have to do is partake of it and sustain it. This is the message of Madinah and the lesson to take home from Madinah. This is that city that gave the sacrifice of life for the hidaayat (guidance) of this Ummat. Should we not also repay this favour in some way? What answer will we have before Allah Ta'ala if our Rabb were to ask us, "I made this *ni'mat* (favour) available so easily for you, did you also convey it to others around you?"

دَعَا إِلَى اللهِ فَالْمُسْتَمْسِكُوْنَ بِهِ مُسْتَمْسِكُوْنَ بِحَبْلٍ غَيْرِ مُنْفَصِمٍ

He ﷺ called (the people) towards Allah (Almighty), so those who cling to him are clinging to a rope which will never break.

Love for Madinah Munawwarah

On our last day before leaving Madinah Munawwarah, Hadhrat Mufti Saahib *(daamat barakaatuhu)* instructed us to buy some dates from the date market to take back home as a *tabarruk* (blessing) of Madinah Shareef. He also mentioned the following inspiring incident of Hadhrat Moulana Badr-e-Aalam Saahib *(rahmatullahi alayh)*.

"Once, a person who was the mureed of Hadhrat Moulana Abdul Qaadir Raipuri *(rahmatullahi alayh)* went to Madinah Munawwarah. During his stay there, he would attend the majlis of Hadhrat Moulana Badr-e-Aalam Saahib *(rahmatullahi alayh)* daily after the Asar Salaah. On one particular day, this person did not attend the majlis. When Hadhrat met him the next day, he asked him why he hadn't attended the program the previous day. To this the person replied, 'I went to purchase the dates of Madinah Munawwarah which I intended to take back home for my family and friends. I am leaving for Makkah Mukarramah tomorrow and I thought I will finish all my work before leaving."

When Hadhrat Moulana Badr-e-Aalam Saahib *(rahmatullahi alayh)* heard this he sighed deeply and mentioned, "Alas, what a pity, due to my ill health I am unable to do much anymore. If only I was young and healthy, I would have definitely accompanied you to the date market and pointed out to you which dates were of a good quality with this intention that when you go back home someone will take this khajoor in his hand and with love for Madinah will say, '*hai Madine ki khajoor*' (Ah! The Khajoor of Madinah) and upon this Allah Ta'ala will make my maghfirat (grant me forgiveness)."

May Allah Ta'ala through His infinite Grace and Mercy bless us with an honourable death of martyrdom in Madinah Munawwarah in a condition that our Rabb is extremely pleased with us. *Aameen.*

کاش ہوتا مدینے میں میرا وطن   پھر مدینے کی لذت میں کیا کہوں

What can I say about the enjoyment in Madinah, How I wish Madinah would be my home land.

خدا سے یہ فریاد کرتے ہیں ہم   مدینے میں ہر سال ہو حاضری

May we be present in Madinah every year, This is what we beg from Allah Ta'ala

خدا سے دعا یہ بھی کرتے ہیں ہم   مدینے میں مرنا مقدر میں ہو

May our passing away be destined in Madinah, This is also what we ask from Allah

Towards Makkah Mukarramah

We put on our ihraam at the hotel, boarded our vehicle and began our journey towards Makkah Mukarramah. Our hearts felt heavy upon leaving the enlightened city. We kept our eyes fixed on the green dome for as long as we could and kept on reciting Durood Shareef. We were now on our way to the mother of all cities, the city of Makkah Mukarramah. How much are the favours of Allah Ta'ala upon us. How is it possible to ever make enough shukar for all that we have? Even a few days in this mubaarak land of Madinah Munawwarah is indeed a GREAT favour of Allah Ta'ala.

Now with our ihraams donned and with the labbaik on our lips, we began moving steadily towards Makkah Mukarramah. This also is such a great favour of Allah Ta'ala. We were now inbetween the two Harams. All praise is due to Allah Ta'ala for this.

صد شکر کہ ہستیم میان دو کریم

Shukar a hundred times (to You, O Allah) that you kept me in between these two places of honour

May Allah Ta'ala accept the journey to Madinah Munawwarah and make it a means of earning His pleasure and the pleasure of Rasulullah ﷺ.

ایں سعادت بزورِ بازو نیست   تا نہ بخشد خدائے بخشندہ

This good fortune is not on account of my efforts, it is the blessings which Allah Ta'ala has blessed me with

Insha Allah we will end this book with a few poems of our elders in praise of Rasulullah ﷺ.

CHAPTER Twelve

Poems in praise of our beloved Nabi ﷺ

1. Arabic Qaseedah

يَاخَيْرَ مَنْ دُفِنَتْ بِالْقَاعِ أَعْظُمُهُ   فَطَابَ مِنْ طِيبِهِنَّ الْقَاعُ وَالْأَكَمُ

O the best of all those who have been buried in the earth, because of which the land and the hills have been blessed.

نَفْسِي الْفِدَاءُ لِقَبْرٍ أَنْتَ سَاكِنُهُ   فِيْهِ الْعَفَافُ وَ فِيْهِ الْجُوْدُ وَالْكَرَمُ

May my life be sacrificed for that grave! Where you are lying, there-in lies virtue, generosity and goodness.

اَنْتَ الشَّفِيْعُ الَّذِيْ تُرْجٰى شَفَاعَتُهُ   عَلَى الصِّرَاطِ اِذَا مَا زَلَّتِ الْقَدَمُ

You are our intercessor whose intercession everyone is hopeful for upon the bridge of siraat when feet shall slip.

وَ صَاحِبَاكَ فَلَا اَنْسَاهُمَا اَبَدًا   مِنِّي السَّلَامُ عَلَيْكُمَا مَا جَرَى الْقَلَمْ

I can never forget your two companions, salaams from me upon you also as long as the pens will write.

فَسَهِّلْ يَا اِلٰهِيْ كُلَّ صَعْبٍ   بِحُرْمَةِ سَيِّدِ الْاَبْرَارِ سَهِّلْ

O Allah, through the blessings of the best of creations, make my hardships and difficulties easy for me.

اِلٰهِيْ نَجِّنِيْ مِنْ كُلِّ ضِيْقٍ   فَاَنْتَ اِلٰهُنَا مَوْلَى الْجَمِيْعِ

O Allah! Save me from every difficulty for You are our Rabb and the Rabb of all.

وَ هَبْ لِيْ فِي الْمَدِيْنَةِ مُسْتَقِرًّا   وَرِزْقًا ثُمَّ دَفْنًا فِي الْبَقِيْعِ

Grant me a place to stay and sustenenace in Madinah and burial in Jannatul Baqee

اَحْسَنَ مِنْكَ لَمْ تَرَ قَطُّ عَيْنِيْ   وَاَجْمَلَ مِنْكَ لَمْ تَلِدِ النِّسَاءُ

Better than you my eye has ever seen, more beautiful than you no woman has given birth to

خُلِقْتَ مُبَرَّءً مِنْ كُلِّ عَيْبٍ   كَاَنَّكَ قَدْ خُلِقْتَ كَمَا تَشَاءُ

You have been created free from any defect, as if you were created like how you desired

Poems regarding Nabi ﷺ

2. Arabic Qaseedah

يَا صَاحِبَ الْجَمَالِ وَيَا سَيِّدَ الْبَشَرْ بِوَجْهِكَ الْمُنِيْرِ لَقَدْ نُوِّرَ الْقَمَرْ

لَا يُمْكِنُ الثَّنَاءُ كَمَا كَانَ حَقُّهٗ بعد از خدا بزرگ توئی قصه مختصر

O the possessor of beauty! O the leader of mankind! By your illuminated countenance has the moon found its light. It is not possible to praise you according to your right. In short, after Allah Ta'ala, you are the greatest and that's it.

طَلَعَ الْبَدْرُ عَلَيْنَا مِنْ ثَنِيَّاتِ الْوَدَاعِ وَجَبَ الشُّكْرُ عَلَيْنَا مَا دَعَا لِلّٰهِ دَاعٍ

*The full moon has risen over us from the mountains of al-Wada'
We shall always give thanks for it, as long as there will be callers to Allah.*

اَيُّهَا الْمَبْعُوْثُ فِيْنَا جِئْتَ بِالْأَمْرِ الْمُطَاعِ

جِئْتَ شَرَّفْتَ الْمَدِيْنَةَ مَرْحَبًا يَا خَيْرَ دَاعٍ

O you who was sent to us! You came with a command to be obeyed. You came to give honour to our city, Welcome O best of callers!

بَلَغَ الْعُلٰى بِكَمَالِهٖ كَشَفَ الدُّجٰى بِجَمَالِهٖ

حَسُنَتْ جَمِيْعُ خِصَالِهٖ صَلُّوْا عَلَيْهِ وَاٰلِهٖ

*He (sallallahu alayhi wasallam) attained eminence by his perfection, the darkness was lifted by his beauty.
Beautiful are all of his qualities, Blessings upon him and his family*

In the City of Rasulullah

3. Arabic Qaseedah

اِنْ نِلْتِ يَا رِيْحَ الصَّبَا يَوْمًا اِلٰى اَرْضِ الْحَرَمْ

بَلِّغْ سَلَامِيْ رَوْضَةً فِيْهَا النَّبِيُّ الْمُحْتَرَمْ

O morning breeze, if you go to the blessed lands, Present my salaam to the grave where Rasulullah (sallallahu alayhi wasallam) rests,

مَنْ وَجْهُهٗ شَمْسُ الضُّحٰى مَنْ خَدُّهٗ بَدْرُ الدُّجٰى

مَنْ ذَاتُهٗ نُوْرُ الْهُدٰى مَنْ كَفُّهٗ بَحْرُ الْهِمَمْ

Whose face is radiant like the sun, whose cheeks are like the full moon, Whose being is the light of guidance, whose hands are oceans of greatness.

Poems regarding Nabi

4. Qaseedah Burdah

مُحَمَّدٌ سَيِّدُ الْكَــوْنَيْنِ وَالثَّقَلَيْنِ   وَالْفَرِيْقَيْنِ مِنْ عُــرْبٍ وَّمِنْ عَجَمِ

(The beloved Prophet) Muhammad ﷺ is the Leader of both the worlds and both the creations (man and jinn) and of both the groups, Arabs and non Arabs.

نَبِيُّنَا الْآمِرُ النَّـاهِيْ فَلَا أَحَـدٌ   أَبَرُّ فِيْ قَـوْلِ لَا مِنْهُ وَلَا نَعَمِ

Our Nabi ﷺ is the one who commands (to do good and) forbids (evil), undoubtedly there is none (parallel to him who is) more truthful than him in saying, "No" or "Yes".

هُوَ الْحَبِيْبُ الَّـذِيْ تُرْجٰى شَفَاعَتُهُ   لِكُــلِّ هَوْلٍ مِّنَ الْأَهْـوَالِ مُقْتَحِمِ

He ﷺ is the most beloved (of Allah Almighty) whose intercession is hoped for every fear (and distress) that is going to come (on the day of agony and fears).

دَعَـا إِلَى اللهِ فَالْمُسْتَمْسِكُوْنَ بِـهِ   مُسْتَمْسِكُوْنَ بِحَبْلٍ غَيْرِ مُنْفَصِمِ

He ﷺ called (the people) towards Allah (Almighty), so those who cling to him are clinging to a rope which will never break.

فَـاقَ النَّبِيِّيْنَ فِيْ خَلْقٍ وَفِيْ خُلُقٍ   وَلَمْ يُدَانُوْهُ فِيْ عِلْـمٍ وَّلَا كَرَمِ

He ﷺ exceeds (transcends) the prophets (عليهم السلام) physically and in noble character; and (none of the other prophets(عليهم السلام) can reach (touch) his knowledge, noble nature and kindness.

In the City of Rasulullah ﷺ

وَانْسُبْ اِلٰى ذَاتِهٖ مَا شِئْتَ مِنْ شَرَفٍ ۞ وَانْسُبْ اِلٰى قَدْرِهٖ مَا شِئْتَ مِنْ عِظَمٖ

And attribute (claim) to his personality whatever you wish to (claim) in (his) excellence; and attribute greatness towards his (highly) dignified status as much as you wish (except committing polytheism).

بُشْرٰى لَنَا مَعْشَرَ الْاِسْلَامِ اِنَّ لَنَا ۞ مِنَ الْعِنَايَةِ رُكْنًا غَيْرَ مُنْهَدِمٖ

(O) People of Islam! Glad tidings be to (all of) us that we have (been bestowed) by the Grace (of Allah Almighty, such a) pillar (which) will never be destroyed.

لَمَّا دَعَى اللهُ دَاعِيْنَا لِطَاعَتِهٖ ۞ بِأَكْرَمِ الرُّسُلِ كُنَّا أَكْرَمَ الْاُمَمٖ

When Allah (Almighty) called (Muhammad ﷺ) who invited us to His worship (who is) the noblest of messengers, (so being noblest) we are the noblest of Ummats.

يَا رَبِّ بِالْمُصْطَفٰى بَلِّغْ مَقَاصِدَنَا ۞ وَاغْفِرْ لَنَا مَامَضٰى يَا وَاسِعَ الْكَرَمٖ

O (Our) Lord! Fulfill (all of) our (good) objectives and forgive us what has passed (in committing sins) for the sake of (Your Beloved Prophet) Mustafa (the chosen one ﷺ), O the Most bountiful (and the most generous).

Poems regarding Nabi ﷺ

5. Urdu Qaseedah

There is one word that is never on your lips, and that is the word NO!

O Rabb! You are Kareem and Rasulullah ﷺ is also kareem (benevolent), how fortunate am I, that I am between two Kareems!

You possess the beauty of Yusuf عَلَيْهِ ٱلسَّلَام, the breath of Isa عَلَيْهِ ٱلسَّلَام, and the bright hand of Musa عَلَيْهِ ٱلسَّلَام, whatever good attributes the greats all have, you ﷺ alone possess.

My heart is restless, when will I reach Madinah?

How fortunate am I, (my good fortune) that I am making Tawaaf of your house. , Am I awake or is this a dream?

In the City of Rasulullah

اے خدا ایں بندہ را رسوا مکن   گر بدم من سر من پیدا مکن

O Allah! Don't disgrace this servant of yours, even though I am a sinner, don't expose my sins

اگرچہ پر خطا ہے پر کہاں جائے تیرا بندہ   تیرے در پر تیرا بندہ با امید کرم آیا

Though I am so sinful O Allah, but where else can I go to? Your slave has come to your doorstep with lots of hope

6. Naat of Hadhrat Qari Siddeeq Ahmad Bandwi (rahmatullahi alayh)

تمنا ہے کہ گلزارِ مدینہ اب وطن ہوتا
وہاں کے گلشنوں میں کوئی اپنا بھی چمن ہوتا

How I wish Madinah was my home, And that I had my own little garden in the gardens of Madinah

بسر اب زندگی اپنی دیارِ قدس میں ہوتی
وہیں جیتا وہیں مرتا وہیں گور و کفن ہوتا

I wish I could pass my life in the sacred land of Madinah, wherein I will live, die and be buried

میسر بال و پر ہوتے تو میں اُڑ کر پہنچ جاتا
زہے قسمت کہ اپنا آشیاں ان کا چمن ہوتا

I wish I had wings, then I would fly to Madinah, And I wish I had the good fortune of having my nest in that garden

یہی ہے آرزو ثاقب یہی اپنی تمنا ہے
کہ پیوندِ بقیعِ پاک اپنا بھی بدن ہوتا

This is my desire, this is my wish that my body be attached to the blessed land of Baqee

7. Urdu Qaseedah of Hadhrat Moulana Qaasim Nanotwi (rahmatullahi alayh)

نہوے نغمہ سرا اس طرح سے بلبل زار

کہ آئی ہے نئے سر سے چمن چمن میں بہار

The nightingale bursts forth in a song of happiness, the freshness of springtime in the garden now prevails.

ہر اک کو حسبِ لیاقت بہار دیتی ہے

کسی کو برگ کسی کو گل اور کسی کو بار

And in accordance with their capability, to some a leaf and to some a rose, to some a fruit

خوشی سے مرغِ چمن ناچ ناچ گاتے ہیں

کفِ ورق سے بجاتے ہیں تالیاں اشجار

Birds of the garden in joyfulness do dance and sing, and the trees shaking their leaves, with clapping applaud

بُجھائی ہے دلِ آتش کی بھی تپش یارب

کرم میں آپ کو دشمن سے بھی نہیں انکار

O You Sustainer of all, who the fire to coolness did command, and not even to an enemy kindness does refuse.

یہ قدرِ خاک ہے، ہیں باغ باغ وہ عاشق
کبھی رہے تھا سدا، جن کے دل کے بیچ غبار

So great Your reward for the lowliest of Your lovers, now jubilant, even though with heavy hearts their days they have passed.

یہ سبزہ زار کا رتبہ ہے شجرۂ موسیٰ
بنا ہے خاص تجلی کا مطلعِ انوار

The green meadows the rank of Moosa's (alayhis salaam) tree have attained. And now the radiance of a special light of Allah reflect.

اسی لئے چمنستان میں رنگِ مہندی نے
کیا ظہور ورق ہائے سبزہ میں ناچار

And thus in the orchard a wealth of colour is seen, as every form of plant life in greenness is clouded.

پہنچ سکے شجر طور کو کہیں طوبیٰ
مقامِ یار کو کب پہنچے مسکنِ اغیار

As the tree of Mount Toor has no likeness to the tree of Tooba in paradise. So the abode of the beloved has no likeness to the abode of an intruder.

زمین و چرخ میں ہو کیوں نہ فرق چرخ و زمیں
یہ سب کا بار اُٹھائے وہ سب کے سر پر بار

As the earth and sky are distant from each other and different, so the earth bears the burden of all, while the sky bears the burden hanging above.

In the City of Rasulullah ﷺ

کرے ہے ذرّہ کوئے محمّدی سے خجل
فلک کے شمس و قمر کو زمین لیل و نہار

The earth belittles the sun and moon by night and day, because of the particles of soil surrounding Muhammad's ﷺ body.

فلک پہ عیسیٰ و ادریس ہیں تو خیر سہی
زمیں پہ جلوہ نما ہیں محمد مختار

In the heavens Isa (alayhis salaam) and Idrees (alayhis salaam) are found, it is true, but here on earth do shine the splendour of Muhammad (sallallahu alayhi wasallam) the great.

فلک پہ سب سہی پر ہے نہ ثانی احمد
زمیں پہ کچھ نہ ہو پر ہے محمدی سرکار

And whether all the heavens are filled they still lack his presence, and even if the earth is empty and Muhammad (sallallahu alayhi wasallam) is there, it's filled indeed!

ثنا کر اس کی فقط قاسم اور سب کو چھوڑ
کہاں کا سبزہ کہاں کا چمن کہاں کی بہار

O Qaasim, praise him alone and discard your praise for others, whose beauty has his ever freshness in a fragrant garden even in the midst of Spring.

الٰہی کس سے بیان ہو سکے ثنا اس کی
کہ جس پہ ایسا تری ذاتِ خاص کا ہو پیار

Poems regarding Nabi

O Allah, who is there that can indeed with adequacy praise him? Him for whom Your being has expressed such infinite love?

جو تو اسے نہ بناتا تو سارے عالم کو

نصیب ہوتی نہ دولتِ وجود کی زنہار

Had you not created him then in truth, not this world nor anything in it would have enjoyed the joy of existence.

کہاں وہ رتبہ کہاں عقلِ نارسا اپنی

کہاں وہ نورِ خدا اور کہاں یہ دیدۂ زار

How can my intellect perceive his exalted rank? How can my limited eyes perceive the light of Allah?

چراغِ عقل ہے گل اس کے نور کے آگے

زباں کا منہ نہیں جو مدح میں کرے گفتار

Before the shine of his light the lamp of my reason died off, and my tongue has not the words to express his worthy praise.

جہاں کہ جلتے ہوں پر عقلِ کل کے بھی پھر کیا

لگی ہے جان جو پہنچیں وہاں مرے افکار

Where even the wings of wisdom lag far behind, and so even my imaginative powers, though soaring high.

مگر کرے مری روح القدس مددگاری
تو اس کی مدح میں میں بھی کروں رقم اشعار

Yet Allah, if Your noble spirit do guide me, then in humbleness I too in his praise would pen down these lines.

جو جبریئیل مدد پر ہو فکر کی میرے
تو آگے بڑھ کے کہوں اے جہاں کے سردار

And while Jibra-eel's (alayhis salaam) helps to stir my thoughts, I shall say unto him, "O Muhammad ﷺ, chosen from amongst all men."

تو فخرِ کون و مکاں زبدۂ زمین و زماں
امیرِ لشکرِ پیغمبراں شہِ ابرار

You are the pride of space and time, the glory of this earth, and you are the leader of the host of Prophets, those truly saintly beings.

تو بوئے گل ہے اگر مثلِ گل ہیں اور نبی
تو نورِ شمس گر اور انبیاء ہیں شمس و نہار

If we compare the Prophets to a rose, you are the fragrance thereof, and if they are the shining sun of the day, you are the rays thereof.

حیاتِ جاں ہے تو ہیں اگر وہ جانِ جہاں
تو نورِ دیدہ ہے گر ہیں وہ دیدۂ بیدار

If they are the life of the world, you are the essence of life, and where they are the sense of sight, you are the light of eyes.

Poems regarding Nabi ﷺ

طفیل آپ کے ہے کائنات کی ہستی
بجا ہے کیسے اگر تم کو مبدء الآثار

Through you has come into existence all that exists, and so be it for you are the first of all creation.

جلوے میں تیرے سب آئے عدم سے تا بوجود
قیامت آپ کی تھی دیکھئے تو اِک رفتار

Through you has all been brought from non-existence into being, that life-giving blessing from you did come.

جہاں کے سارے کمالات ایک تجھ میں ہیں
ترے کمال کسی میں نہیں مگر دو چار

All the excellence of this world in you is found, and except for one or two, your merits are found in none.

پہنچ سکا ترے رتبہ تلک نہ کوئی نبی
ہوئے ہیں معجزہ والے بھی اس جگہ ناچار

Not one Nabi could ever reach to your noble rank, even though among them workers of miracles are found.

جو انبیاء ہیں وہ آگے تری نبوت کے
کریں ہیں امتی ہونے کا یا نبی اقرار

And every Nabi shall express belief in your Nubuwwat and a follower of your mission shall he be.

In the City of Rasulullah ﷺ

لگا تا ہاتھ نہ پیلے کو بوالبشر کے خدا

اگر ظہور نہ ہوتا تمہارا آخرِ کار

Never would Allah have looked upon Aadam (alayhis salaam) had your appearance not been made at last.

خدا کے طالبِ دیدار حضرت موسیٰ

تمہارا ایسے، خدا آپ طالبِ دیدار

Moosa (alayhis salaam) was indeed desirous of seeing Allah Ta'ala, and behold with you, Allah Himself was desirous of meeting you.

کہاں بلندیٔ طور اور کہاں تری معراج

کہیں ہوئے ہیں زمین آسمان بھی ہموار

How can the heights of Mount Toor compare with the heights of your meraaj (ascension), has the heavens and the earth ever been traversed as with you?

جمال کو ترے کب پہنچے حسنِ یوسف کا

وہ دلرُبائے زلیخا تو شاہدِ ستار

Never will the beauty of Yusuf عَلَيْهِ السَّلَام approach your shining countenance, even though Zulaikha had been bewitched thereby.

رہا جمال پہ تیرے حجابِ بشریّت

نجانا کون ہے کچھ بھی کسی نے جز ستار

Your glory had the veil of humanity over it, so none except Allah Ta'ala could discern your total reality.

Poems regarding Nabi ﷺ

سما سکے تری خلوت میں کب نبی و ملک
خدا غیور تو اُس کا حبیب اور اغیار

Neither Prophet nor angel could intrude into your seclusion with Allah, and you are His beloved so all others are mere outsiders.

نہ بن پڑا وہ جمال آپ کا سا اک شب بھی
قمر نے گو کہ کروڑوں کیئے چڑھاؤ اتار

The moon could not attain to your beauty even for one night, although it went into millions of revolutions.

خوشا نصیب یہ نسبت کہاں نصیب مرے
تو جس قدر ہے بھلا میں برا اسی مقدار

To my good fortune I have a likeness with you, that in similar measure as you are good, so am I weak.

نہ پہنچیں گنتی میں ہر گز ترے کمالوں کی
مرے بھی عیب شہِ دو سرا شہِ ابرار

Never can the sum of my defects be equal to the total of your virtues, O leader of both worlds, and king of virtuous ones.

عجب نہیں تری خاطر سے تیری امت کے
گناہ ہوویں قیامت کو طاعتوں میں شمار

No wonder on the day of Judgement, the sins of your followers will be counted as obedience for your sake.

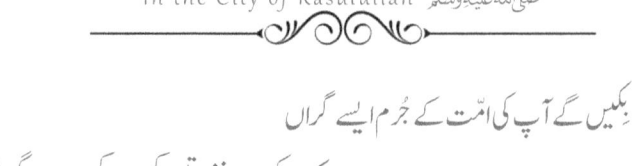

بِکیں گے آپ کی اُمّت کے جُرم ایسے گراں
کہ لاکھوں مغفرتیں کم سے کم پہ ہوں گی نثار

So high will the sins of your Ummat be valued that tons of pardon be lavishly granted to a few of them.

ترے بھروسہ پہ رکھتا ہے غرۂ طاعت
گناہِ قاسم بر گشتہ بخت بد اطوار

So ill-fated and sinful, this Qaasim hopefully relies on you, that through you his sins be changed to acts of obedience.

تمہارے حرفِ شفاعت پہ عفو ہے عاشق
اگر گناہ کو ہے خوفِ غصہ قہّار

When sinners fear the wrath of Allah, Most Great, a mere word of intercession from you brings forgiveness and pardon.

یہ سُن کے آپ شفیعِ گناہ گاراں ہیں
کیئے ہیں میں نے اکٹھے گناہ کے انبار

Having heard that on behalf of sinners you will intercede, have I gathered piles of sins, to be forgiven.

ترے لحاظ سے اتنی تو ہو گی تخفیف
بشر گناہ کریں اور ملائک استغفار

Out of consideration for you, this favour is granted, that while men do sins, Angels pray for their forgiveness.

Poems regarding Nabi ﷺ

یہ ہے اجابتِ حق کو تری دعا کا لحاظ
قضائے مبرم و مشروط کی سنیں نہ پکار

So well is Allah disposed to your prayers that even conditional fates voice is stilled.

براہوں، بدہوں، گنہگار ہوں پہ تیرا ہوں
ترا کہیں ہیں مجھے گو کہ ہوں میں ناہنجار

Sinful even though I am, yet I remain yours, so am I known, though worthless I am.

لگے ہے تیرے سگ کو کو میرے نام سے عیب
پہ تیرے نام کا لگنا مجھے ہے عزّ و قار

It would be insulting to you that your dog should bear my name, but an honour to me to be so connected with you.

تو بہترین خلائق، میں بدترین جہاں
تو سرورِ دو جہاں، میں کمینہ خدمتگار

While the best of creation you are, the worst am I, and while master of both worlds you are, the lowest am I.

بہت دنوں سے تمنا ہے کیجے عرضِ حال
اگر ہو اپنا کسی طرح تیرے در تک بار

For years have I longed to open to you my heart, if ever I get a chance to reach your Raudha.

In the City of Rasulullah ﷺ

مگر جہاں ہو فلک آستاں سے بھی نیچا
وہاں ہو قاسمؔ بے بال و پر کا کیونکہ گزار

But where even the heaven is lower than your threshold, there is it most difficult for Qaasim to find a way.

دیا ہے حق نے تجھے سب سے مرتبہ عالی
کیا ہے سارے بڑے چھوٹوں کا تجھے سردار

The highest rank did Allah graciously grant unto you, and to be chief over all has He elevated you.

جو تو ہی ہم کو نہ پوچھے تو کون پوچھے گا
بنے گا کون ہمارا ترے سوا غم خوار

If you do not care for us, then who shall? And who besides you, can truly console us all?

لیا ہے سگ نما ابلیس نے مرا پیچھا
ہوا ہے نفس موا سانپ سا گلے کا ہار

Indeed does shaytaan constantly pursue me like a dog, and my nafs (carnal self) hangs around my neck like a snake.

رجاؤ خوف کی موجوں میں ہے، امید کی ناؤ
کہ ہو سگانِ مدینہ میں میرا نام شمار

In huge waves of hope and fear the boat of my future lies, hoping that I may be counted among the obedient dogs of Madinah.

Poems regarding Nabi ﷺ

جیوں تو ساتھ سگانِ حرم کے تیرے پھروں

مروں تو کھائیں مدینہ کے مجھ کو مور و مار

I hope that among the dogs of your sacred haram I shall roam, till the end of my days, and that I be eaten by the ants and snakes of Madinah.

اُڑا کے باد مری مشتِ خاک کو پسِ مرگ

کرے حضور کے روضہ کے آس پاس نثار

And I hope that on having turned to dust at death, the wind shall spread my dust over the Rowdha Mubarak.

ولے یہ رتبہ کہاں مُشتِ خاکِ قاسم کا

کہ جائے کوچۂ اطہر میں تیرے بن کے غبار

Alas, the earthly remains of Qaasim can hardly reach that holy place even in the shape of dust.

غرض نہیں مجھے اس سے بھی کچھ رہی لیکن

خدا کی اور تری الفت سے میرا سینہ فگار

About other things I care not much, except that forever my heart be sore with love for Allah and for you.

لگے وہ تیرِ غمِ عشق کا مرے دل میں

ہزار پارہ ہو دل خونِ دل میں ہو سرشار

And I wish that such an arrow pierces and breaks my heart into a thousand pieces, still delighted while shedding blood.

In the City of Rasulullah ﷺ

لگے وہ آتشِ عشق اپنی جان میں جس کی
جلا دے چرخِ ستم گر کو ایک ہی جھونکار

That my soul be filled with such burning love, which, in one blaze, burn down the oppressive sky.

تمہارے عشق میں رو رو کے ہوں نحیف اتنا
کہ آنکھیں چشمۂ آبی سے ہوں درونِ غبار

May it then be that through my love for you so much I weep, that weak in my body I become, and my eyes be like fountains shedding tears.

رہے نہ منصبِ شیخُ المشائخی کی طلب
نہ جی کو بھائے یہ دنیا کا کچھ بناؤ سنگار

Then no aspiration will remain in me to spiritual heights, and for me the adornment of the world will have no charm.

ہوا اشارہ میں دو ٹکڑے جوں قمر کا جگر
کوئی اشارہ ہمارے بھی دل کے ہو جا پار

Through a sign from you the moon was split in two, and now we look for a gesture to cleave our hearts.

تو تھام اپنے تئیں حد سے پا نہ دھر باہر
سنبھال اپنے تئیں اور سنبھل کے کر گفتار

And O Qaasim, now you compose yourself and step not beyond bounds, and withhold yourself while talking in a cautious way.

Poems regarding Nabi ﷺ

ادب کی جا ہے یہ چُپ ہو تو اور زبان بند کر
وہ جانے چھوڑ اسے پر نہ کر تو کچھ اصرار

For this is a spot that silence and respect demands, so silence do give.

بس اب دُرود پڑھ اُس پر اور اُس کی آل پہ تو
جو خوش ہو تجھ سے وہ، اور اس کی عترتِ اطہار

Send only salaat on him (durood) and his descendants, that he and his progeny will be pleased with you.

الٰہی اس پر اور اس کی تمام آل پہ بھیج
وہ رحمتیں کہ عدد کر سکے نہ ان کو شمار

O Allah! send upon Rasulullah ﷺ and all his family such blessings that cannot be counted.

8. Masnawi of Mulla Jaami (rahmatullahi alayh)

ترحّم یا نبی اللہ ترحّم   ز مہجوری برآمد جانِ عالم

O Rasul of Allah ﷺ, the seal of Prophethood, bestow your generous attention (upon us), for greatly bereaved is the world since your demise.

ز محرومان چرا غافل نشینی   نہ آخر رحمۃ للعالمینی

Are you not indeed the last of the messengers and their seal. Thus it is not possible for you to then ignore us in this pitiable plight?

خواب چند از خواب برخیز   ز خاک اے لالۂ سیراب برخیز چو نرگس

O dearest one, through your evergreen freshness, grace this world now and attend to us from the depths of your absorption (in the love of Allah Ta'ala) filling us with guiding light.

کہ روے تست صبح زندگانی   بروں آور سر از بردِ یمانی

Lift your blessed countenance from within your Yemeni shroud, for your blessed face is the beginning of life and is the light of the day.

ز رویت روز ما فیروز گرداں   شبِ اندوہِ ما را روز گرداں

Turn the darkness of our sorrowful night into the radiance of a bright day, and crown this day of ours with success.

بسر بربند کافوری عمامہ   بہ تن در پوش عنبر بوے جامہ

(O Rasul of Allah ﷺ) Don your fragrant garments, and place on your blessed head the white turban

Poems regarding Nabi ﷺ

فرود آویز از سرِ گیسواں را نگن سایہ بپا سر درواں را

Allow your dark and precious locks of hair to hang down so that their shade may fall upon your blessed feet.

ادیم طائفے نعلین پاکن شراک از رشتہ جانہائے ما کن

Wrap your feet in your shoes from the hills of Taa'if and make your straps bind our souls.

جہاں نے دیدہ کردہ فرشِ راہ اند چو فرشِ اقبال پابوس تو خواہند

This entire universe desires to be spread at your feet, and sincerely wishes for your honourable steps.

ز حجرہ پائے در صحنِ حرم نہ بفرقِ خاکِ رہ بوساں قدم نہ

Come forth from your Raudha Mubaarak into the Nabawi ﷺ Masjid, so that we may kiss and lay our heads on the dust under your feet where you tread.

بدہ دستی زپا افتادگاں را بکن دلداریئے دلدادگاں را

O Rasulullah ﷺ, grant refuge and help to the needy and console the hearts of those filled with love for you.

اگرچہ غرق دریائے گناہم فتادہ خشک لب بر خاک راہم

Indeed we are sinners, drowned in the sea of our sins. Yet great is the thirst of our endeavour to follow your way.

تو ابرِ رحمتی آں بہ کہ گاہے کنی بر حالِ لبِ خشکاں نگاہے

You are the rain cloud of mercy and your generosity demands that help be granted to the thirsty seeker in search of you.

In the City of Rasulullah

How wonderful would be that day when to your abode I shall come and blacken my eyes with the dust of Madinah. (May Allah Ta'ala hasten that day of my arrival in Madinah, to refresh my eyes with the dust of Madinah).

How wonderful would be that day, when after performing the salaah of thanks and the sajdah of thanks, my soul shall fly into the midst of the sacred Raudha?

When in loving madness, overjoyed heart and overflowing yearning, I shall walk amidst your grave and the Green Dome.

How glorious would be that day when from the clouds of my eyes, raindrops of tears shall sprinkle upon the threshold of your Haram and your grave.

When in joyful bliss I shall feel blessed to sweep away the dust of your Haram in ecstasy, to remove all the dust from around you.

Though dust be hurtful to the eyes, yet your dust is a light and cure for me, and though litter is of no benefit to wounds, to me the litter of Madinah shall be a perfect cure for the ills of my heart.

To your honoured mimbar shall I go and rubbing thereupon my face, which will go pale out of love for you, hoping that it shall become golden.

Poems regarding Nabi ﷺ

ز محرابت بسجده کام جستیم قدم گاہت بخون دیدہ شستیم

Then (I shall go) to your musalla and your mimbar to stand in salaah fulfilling my hearts desires. Standing where you once stood, to wash your footsteps in the streams of my blood (of love).

بپائے ہر ستوں قد راست کردیم مقام راستاں درخواست کردیم

Then to every pillar of your Masjid I will stand in utmost humbleness. Begging of Allah Ta'ala for faith and the ranks of the Siddiq.

ز داغ آرزویت بادل خوش زدیم از دل بہر قندیل آتش

Indeed will the great hopes and desires of my heart in extreme pleasure, cause every candle on earth to glow most brightly.

کنوں گرتن نہ خاک آں حریم است بحمد اللہ کہ جاں آں جا مقیم است

Though my body does not appear in your presence as yet, grateful am I to Allah Ta'ala that my soul is there for me.

بخود درماندہ ام از نفس خود رائے ببیں درماندہ را چندیں ببخشائے

O Rasulullah ﷺ, frustrated have I become, dejected of my selfishness. Help this helpless soul and turn your gaze of favour towards him.

اگر نبود چو لطفت دست یارے زدست ما نیاید ہیچ کارے

If your loving kindness is not showered upon us, paralysis would overtake us and defeated shall we be.

قضامی افگند از راہ مارا خدا را از خدا درخواہ مارا

Our ill-fate has turned us from Allah's path of righteousness. You make dua to Him on our behalf for complete guidance.

کہ بخشد از یقین اوّل حیاتے   دہد آنگہ بکار دیں ثباتے

(This dua was then said), O Allah, firstly grant us true faith in a goodly, fruitful life. And guide us, O Allah, to be steadfast in following the Deen.

چو ہول روز رستاخیز خیزد   بآتش آبرد ے ما نیز د

When we meet the terrors of Qiyaamah, the Rabb of the day of Qiyaamah shall save us from it with honour and dignity.

کند باایں ہمہ گمراہی ما   ترا از ان شفاعت خواہی ما

In spite of our numerous heinous sins, Allah Ta'ala shall grant Hadhrat Muhammadﷺ, the power to intercede for us, without which we will be lost.

چو چوگاں سر فگندہ آ دری روے   بمیدان شفاعت امّتی گوے

You shall arrive on the plains of reckoning, while we, encircled by our sins shall look on as you shall bend your head in dua, calling out, "Forgive my Ummat, O Allah! Forgive them."

بحسنِ اہتمامت کار جامی   طفیل دیگراں یا بد تمامی

And may through your glorious efforts and the blessings of the pious, this Jaami also be included amongst the accepted and pardoned ones. Aameen.

Poems regarding Nabi ﷺ

مدح النبي صلى الله عليه وسلم[1]

تیری شان خاکساری	تیری ہر ادا ہے پیاری

تیری زلفِ عنبریں پر   ہو نثار بے قراری
تیرے در کی خاک روبی   سے ملی ہمیں مسرّت
تیرے ہر زماں زمیں میں   ہے گلاب جیسی نکہت
تیرے جلوۂ حسیں سے   ہے خمار سب پہ طاری

تیری شان خاکساری	تیری ہر ادا ہے پیاری

تو ہدایتوں کا پیکر   تو ہے رحمتِ مجسم
تو ہے زندگی کا رہبر   تو دکھے دلوں کا مرہم
شب و روز یہ دعائیں   کوئی رہ نہ جائے ناری

تیری ہر ادا ہے پیاری	تیری ہر ادا ہے پیاری

---

[1] This naat has been compiled by Hadhrat Mufti Radhaul Haq Saahib (db)

In the City of Rasulullah ﷺ

تو سخاوتوں کا مرکز
تو شرافتوں کا معدن
تیری ذات اونچی پھر بھی

تو ہے انبیاء کا خاتم
ہو درود تجھ پہ ہر دم
تیری شان انکساری

تیری ہر ادا ہے پیاری

تیری شان خاکساری

تو ستائشوں کے قابل
مرے دل کی دھڑکنوں میں
تیری یاد کی جوانی

تیرا ذکر میرا فن ہے
شب و روز مو جزن ہے
سے دلوں کی آبیاری

تیری ہر ادا ہے پیاری

تیری شان خاکساری

ذرا دیکھ لو مدینہ
یہ تلاوتوں کی محفل
کوئی رو رہا ہے پیارا

یہاں رحمتوں کے بادل
یہ عبادتوں کی منزل
ہے درود لب پہ جاری

تیری ہر ادا ہے پیاری

تیری شان خاکساری

Poems regarding Nabi ﷺ

شہِ دو جہاں کے پیارا	میں کیا کہوں صحابہ
وہی دین کے ستارے	وہی یار ہیں نبی کے
وہ قرآن کے تھے قاری	ہے بلند ان کا رتبہ

تیری شان خاکساری	تیری ہر ادا ہے پیاری

کہیں لگ گئی ہیں نظریں	اسی امّت نبیؐ کو
یہی آرہی ہیں خبریں	جو تھی ایک, لڑ رہی ہے
کبھی دوسرے کا باری	کبھی ایک پٹ رہا ہے

تیری شان خاکساری	تیری ہر ادا ہے پیاری

تیری مدحتیں میرا فن	تیرا نام ہے محمد صلی اللہ علیہ وسلم
میری شاعری کی دھڑکن	ہو نثار تجھ پہ آقا
تیرے دیں پہ جاں نثاری	ہے رضاؔ کی بس تمنّا

تیری شان خاکساری	تیری ہر ادا ہے پیاری

www.ingramcontent.com/pod-product-compliance
Lightning Source LLC
LaVergne TN
LVHW011935070526
838202LV00054B/4648